CW00816418

BUILDING WEALTH

THROUGH

INVESTMENT PROPERTY

by

Jan Somers

The laws relating to property investment are complex and constantly changing. Every effort has been made to ensure that this book is free from errors. No responsibility can be accepted by either the author or printer for any action taken by any persons or organisations, relating to material in this book. All persons should satisfy themselves independently as to the relevancy of the material to their own particular situation.

Published by:

Somerset Financial Services Pty Ltd

PO Box 615

Cleveland Qld. 4163.

Telephone: (07) 3286 4368

Fax: (07) 3821 2005

First Released February, 1992

Reprinted April, 1992

Reprinted July, 1992

Reprinted October, 1992

Reprinted July, 1993

Reprinted April, 1994

Reprinted December, 1994

Reprinted January, 1996

Reprinted May, 1997

Printed in Brisbane by Inprint Ltd

Distributed by Herron Book Distributors

Copyright 1992, J.B. Somers of Somerset Financial Services Pty Ltd

A.C.N. 058 152 337

National Library of Australia

Cataloguing-in-Publication Data.

ISBN 0 646 06896 2

Acknowledgement

A special thank you to my husband Ian for his help and understanding, to my children Will, Tom, and Bonnie for their patience and to my mother for her countless cups of tea.

CONTENTS

INTRODUCTION

The aim of this book is to show you how to build wealth through long-term investment in residential rental property. In essence, this is achieved by diverting some of your short-term income into long-term asset building. But don't be mislead - it's not a "get-rich-quick-scheme", nor are the principles it follows new, but it is the surest path to personal wealth I know. In fact, herein is a recipe for a personal superannuation scheme that will offer far better returns and much greater flexibility than any normal institutional superannuation scheme. How can this be so? Does property investment offer the same tax advantages that are the supposed attractions of normal superannuation? And how much do you need to get started?

As the ensuing chapters will explain, residential property has shown consistent returns above inflation over the longer term, which is more than can be claimed for many other forms of investments. Suitably financed, property investment offers special tax benefits that effectively subsidise your retirement savings. Perhaps best of all, there are no complicated and constantly changing rules governing how you can eventually get your money out of property. There are no lump sum regulations, no reasonable benefits limits, and no age barriers – none of the straightjackets of normal institutional superannuation schemes. You retain control of your own investment – an investment as secure as bricks and mortar.

So why haven't more people discovered property investment? Sadly, our education system does not teach people how to manage their financial affairs. The emphasis is on learning skills to earn money, not on money-management skills which lead to long-term security. Despite a growing awareness of investment products, direct property investment receives scant attention, possibly because many financial advisors tend to be much more aligned to the commissions they receive, than to the independence of their advice. Also, most people are not aware that they can afford to invest in property. They think they need about $100,000 to enter the property market, when in fact, it may take less than $100 a week to get started.

Of course, new players in property investment need help. But where can they find it? People often seek "independent" financial advice from bank managers, accountants and solicitors. But ask yourself this question. If you wanted to be the best cricketer, who would you ask for advice? The promoter who handles the money? The scorekeeper who counts the runs and keeps the score. The umpire who ensures the game is played to the rules? Or would you ask Sir Donald Bradman, the experienced player?

Clearly, if you want to be a successful property investor, you can't rely solely on the advice of the bank manager who just handles the money, nor the accountant who does the sums and keeps score, nor the solicitor who ensures you keep to the rules. You should be seeking the advice of experienced, successful property investors. Bank managers, accountants and solicitors provide expert professional services in the areas in which they are qualified – which is not necessarily property investment. This book, however, is the culmination of 20 years of research and experience in property investment, so you will be learning first hand, how to build wealth through investment property.

The Philosophy

To build a property portfolio, you need to formulate and stick with a consistent investment strategy. The formula developed in this book is to buy income-producing residential investment property that is appropriately financed to achieve maximum tax benefits while you are still working. As property values increase, you continue to refinance so that your liabilities (your borrowings or debt) increase with your assets. You'll then have the opportunity to retire much earlier than would otherwise be possible, at which time you reduce your liabilities by selling a property or two.

This ultimately provides you with a retirement package of residential properties that will continue to grow in value and produce a regular indexed income. In effect, you will be creating your own superannuation fund, but with returns that, in our experience and that of many others, outperform all other investments over the long-term.

The concept of "buying to keep" is difficult for many people to accept because they believe the only way to make a profit is to buy and sell. But you don't have to sell to make a profit. By keeping the property you can then re-invest in more property and put your profit back to work.

Too many investors enter the market with a short-term view that is reinforced by a "myopic media" who report a myriad of short-term crises to sell papers. However, long-term investment in property is relatively unaffected by down-turns in the economy, high interest rates, fuel crises, and high unemployment. Evidence of this is that in Australia for the last 30 years, capital growth has averaged more than 10% per year compound and has consistently kept ahead of inflation.

For short-term property traders, negotiating a bargain price, finding the best interest rate and deciding when to buy and when to sell are extremely important. With long-term property investment, initial price, interest rates and timing are of less consequence because of the levelling effect of time. Thus, the best time to invest in income-producing residential property is *today*. Time is always on your side.

Summary

The ensuing chapters show you some of the basic steps involved in achieving total financial security through residential investment property.

PART I – Preparing a Blueprint for Wealth establishes the reasons for starting a wealth-building program and looks at the principles of building wealth.

- Chapter 1 looks at the reasons for needing or wanting to acquire wealth and establishes that the basis of true wealth is in property.

- Chapter 2 examines the attitudes, information and skills you'll need to build wealth.

PART II – Laying the Foundations of Wealth provides the evidence supporting the choice of long-term residential property investment.

- Chapter 3 documents the historical information relating to the capital growth and rental income from residential property over a thirty-year period.

- Chapter 4 re-assures us of the wisdom of selecting property, by comparing the attributes of the three basic investment types: cash, shares and property.

- Chapter 5 compares direct property investment with managed investments, especially institutional superannuation products, and shows that over the long term, property provides better returns and greater flexibility.

- Chapter 6 describes our reasons for choosing residential property rather than commercial property or vacant land. It also presents compelling reports by leading research organisations as to the soundness of residential investment property.

- Chapter 7 describes the choices available in residential property and suggests the criteria for choosing a suitable rental property.

- Chapter 8 details the arguments in favour of buying for keeps, rather than trading in property.

PART III – The Framework for Building Wealth outlines the process of building wealth through residential property investment. It provides a strategy for success based on borrowing against existing assets to invest in property without the need for cash deposits.

- Chapter 9 shows you how to get started by buying your first property. It may be your own home or perhaps your circumstances might even enable you to buy an investment property first.

- Chapter 10 describes the method by which you go on from your first home to build a whole portfolio of investment properties. This section gives an example of how a typical couple with a combined income of $45,000 a year can easily build a million dollar property portfolio over the course of 10 years or less.

PART IV – The Tools for Building Wealth explains how to best use the two most important tools – finance and taxation. These chapters provide all the information you'll need to organise your finances in a way that will accelerate your progress toward financial freedom.

- Chapter 11 rationalises the way to make the most of your borrowings through the use of mortgages.
- Chapter 12 details the costs of borrowing including interest rates and establishment fees and explains why interest rates are not the only criterion for selecting a particular type of loan.
- Chapter 13 examines the sources of finance with the aim of helping you choose the best for your circumstance.
- Chapter 14 details the costs in buying and selling, and also explains why the capital gains tax shouldn't discourage you from investing long-term in property.
- Chapter 15 lists the tax deductions that apply to income-producing investment property to help you include everything to which you are entitled.
- Chapter 16 explains the principle of negative gearing and shows you how to receive immediate tax benefits by having your PAYE tax instalments reduced.

PART V – The Maintenance of Wealth completes the picture of how to perpetuate the wealth you have built by managing both your property and finances, and emphasises the importance of learning from others.

- Chapter 17 shows you how to manage your finances. Debt management plays a most important role in successfully maintaining both your property and your wealth.
- Chapter 18 shows you how to manage both your property and the tenants.
- Chapter 19 answers the most commonly asked questions about property investment.
- Chapter 20 provides an annotated bibliography on the subject of building wealth through investment property; recommendations are made concerning some of the more worthwhile books.

PART I

Preparing a Blueprint for Wealth

1
About Wealth

You've just had a hard day at work and arrive home hungry and tired. No one's done anything about organising dinner, so it'll take at least an hour or more to get something nice ready. And then, someone suggests a hamburger and chips at the local fast-food outlet. Sounds like a great idea and off you go. Later that night, with a queasy tummy from all that fatty food, you're beginning to wish you'd waited for those steamed vegies. Sound familiar? You might well ask what fast food has to do with wealth? In principle – everything!

Fast food and instant lotto tickets are characteristics of today's society that seems preoccupied with instant results. We constantly exhaust ourselves looking for a quick and easy way to riches, but spend very little energy on learning the principles of building wealth. Consequently, all the "get-rich-quick-schemes" and gambling games that are aimed at taking advantage of our hunger for riches are overwhelmingly patronised, despite the fact that so few people win anything at all.

Groucho Marx gave us an enlightened view of money. He said:

"It frees you from doing the things you dislike. Since I dislike doing nearly everything, money is handy."

I'm sure you recognise some truth in this statement. It's the reason we want wealth in the first place. Wealth gives us financial freedom. But most of us have the same attitude to wealth as we do to fast food. I want it now, I must have it now – I can't possibly wait. Yet as time goes on, we realise that waiting for our food would have been far healthier – and waiting for our wealth will make us far wealthier.

However, the slower but surer paths to riches are rarely followed. Perhaps patience is a lost virtue, but it's patience you need to build real wealth. What are these tried and true methods and why do so few people take the time to find out about them? What is *real* wealth and why should you bother about it now anyway? If you'd like to know more about how average income earners can achieve long-term financial independence, then read on.

Why become Wealthy?

I don't have to remind you what wealth can do for you. You can have that dream house you've always wanted, private hospitals when you need them, a new car whenever you desire, and overseas holidays whenever you like. I'm sure you'd have no trouble dreaming up what you could spend your money on if you were wealthy.

But perhaps most importantly, it gives you the freedom to choose *when* you retire – that is, choosing when to stop doing what you have to do and to start doing what you want to do.

Of course, some people earnestly believe that it is quite wrong to desire wealth. Usually these same people are keen to give whatever they can to the poor. Think then, how generously you could give to all those in need, if you had real wealth. Your success can help many people – your failure helps no one.

Many people think: "My income gets me by. Why not spend it on all these things I want and enjoy it now? I can always start saving for retirement later and if I fail, the pension will be there." This type of thinking is a trap. It keeps you dependent on your job, dependent on good health, and eventually dependent on the government.

Ask yourselves honestly. Do *you* think there will still be a pension by early next century and if so, will it be enough to pay for the lifestyle you want? – I don't! Today, the pension provides little more than food on the table.

But let's look at what might happen to the aged pension in the future. Australia is faced with an ageing population. In 1920, less than 4% of the population was aged over 65. By 1980, it was 11%, and it's been predicted that by the year 2020, when many of you are thinking of retirement, a massive 18% of the population will be over 65. And by then, there could be one welfare recipient for every taxpayer!

Even today, a staggering 77% of people aged over 65 years are on the pension, each trying to survive on a mere $6,000 to $7,000 a year. The medical technology that helps us live longer has far outpaced society's willingness and the government's ability to pay for an ageing population at anything but a low subsistence level. Unless retirees begin to support themselves, there will be a drastic decline in living standards both for the pensioners, and for the rest of the population who are paying the tax bill.

That's food for thought, isn't it? So we really must alter our way of thinking and begin to accept responsibility for our own financial security. Only wealth can give you total financial security. Wouldn't you like to not have to worry about surviving on the pension?

Who becomes Wealthy?

When it comes to investing, the path of minimal resistance is to do nothing or rely on Lady Luck. But building wealth should not be left to chance. Indeed, statistics show that most people take no positive action to acquire wealth. If we followed the lives of 100 young people today, to see what their circumstances would be by the age of 65, we'd find that:

- **24** would be dead, usually by avoidable causes, because the life expectancy of the average Australian is now 76 years of age.

- Another **54** would be on a Government pension of around $7,000 per year (in today's dollars)– but I'd hardly call that a wealthy prospect.

- **16** would still be working – mostly because they have to, not because they want to. How many older people do you know who simply can't afford to stop working?

- There would be **5** financially independent. They have just enough to support themselves. They can afford to have that interstate holiday once a year and buy a few luxuries. But, they still need to watch their money very carefully to remain financially independent.

- But only **one** of those 100 people would become wealthy. Only 1% would have the ability to do whatever they want, whenever they want.

Wouldn't *you* like to be part of that 1%? Wouldn't *you* like to have whatever you want, whenever you want it? Now I must point out that I am not talking about 1% becoming millionaires. Today, this 1% of people have probably accumulated around $600,000 in net worth – millionaires represent only 0.25% of the population – or in other words, one in 400 people.

It is not the aim of this book to convince everyone that he or she has to become a multi-millionaire to gain financial independence. Rather, it is my aim to show average people the principles of building wealth so that they have the option of acquiring as much as they wish, without having to rely on Lady Luck. If you want to aim for more or less, the principles will be exactly the same.

Many people have at least taken a step in the right direction and have a house, a car, and say, about $200,000 in superannuation at retirement. Unfortunately these people have a false sense of security in believing that a few hundred thousand dollars will make them wealthy.

In fact, they are far from wealthy. If you think $200,000 is adequate for a comfortable retirement, I would like to show you what would happen to your $200,000 if it was invested at 10% before tax (7.5% after-tax) and spent at the rate of $23,000 a year. This should allow you to maintain your present comfortable lifestyle, help with the grandchildren and buy a few luxuries for yourself. Do you know how long your money will last? It would completely run out in just nine years. This period is very short because inflation of 8% per year would be eroding what you can buy (see chapter 3 for CPI figures). You can see from the table below just how this happens.

How Long Will $200,000 Last?

Year	Capital Remaining	After-Tax Income (7.5%)	Living Expenses (rising by 8%)
0	200,000	15,000	23,000
1	192,000	14,400	24,840
2	181,560	13,617	26,827
3	168,350	12,626	28,973
4	152,003	11,400	31,291
5	132,112	9,908	33,795
6	108,225	8,117	36,498
7	79,844	5,988	39,418
8	46,415	3,481	42,571
9	7,324	549	45,977
10	-38,103	-3,334	49,655

After nine years, more money would be spent than there is left in the bank! What usually happens is that everything is fine and rosy for the first few years and you can see by the table, that after four years, much of the money is still "in the bank". But from this point on, the money disappears rapidly.

It is at this stage that the unfortunate retiree realises that he can no longer afford to be a free-spending retiree and must either return to the workforce or accept a greatly reduced standard of living. I'm sure you know many people who have gone back to work after they've retired, simply because they needed more money to keep paying for their normal lifestyle.

Even if you think you'll be OK because you're going to get $500,000 when you retire, I'd like to point out that by the year 2000, the average male earnings could be around $60,000 a year. By then, your $500,000 would still last less than 10 years (see chapter 3 to find out just how fast the male average earnings and CPI have risen over the last 30 years). It's easy to see why a few hundred thousand dollars in the bank does not give you total financial security and cannot be deemed a wealthy amount.

And yet you don't need to become a millionaire to be wealthy, but you certainly need something more than a few hundred thousand dollars if you want to be part of that wealthy 1%. Just how much you need depends on what you want from life, however, there is no reason to settle for less than you want.

The following table should give you a broad picture of the assets you would need, over and above your own home, if you retired *today*. If you are thinking of retiring in 10 years time, you will need roughly double these amounts to enjoy the same standard of living. But remember that individual circumstances are very different and what might be excessive to someone, will be insufficient to someone else.

How Much Is Enough Today?

"Nest Egg"	Comfort Level
Less than $200,000	You will definitely need to supplement your income either with a part pension or part-time work to have a comfortable lifestyle.
$200,000 to $350,000	This may be adequate for basic needs, but to enjoy some of the niceties of life, you'll need to work part-time.
$350,000 to $600,000	You will be one of the five percent who is financially independent, but you will still need to watch what you spend.
$600,000 to $1,000,000	Congratulations to you if you can achieve this level. You will be part of that one percent who is wealthy and have total financial freedom.
More than $1,000,000	You will be one of a rare breed. One in 400 in fact. It's time to enjoy your wealth. You've earned it.

How is Wealth Measured?

Our ideas of wealth are based on false assumptions that we "learn" in early childhood. We are lead to believe that wealthy people must *look* rich and that people who look rich must be wealthy. Nothing could be further from the truth, and this book should dispel this myth about wealth.

This mistaken belief that wealth is manifested in external appearances is the reason we love to surround ourselves with the trappings of wealth in the hope that we will appear wealthy. Nice clothes, luxury cars, grand holidays and expensive furniture are all too often mistaken as a signature of wealth.

However, unless there is an underlying foundation of wealth, all the exterior facade will be lost in time. How many people do you know who appear wealthy and yet own nothing? Their designer suits were bought with plastic money and their flashy cars with personal loans. Wealth by association with external affluence is not a true indication of real wealth at all.

Another misconception is the idea that getting a highly paid job will automatically make us wealthy. However, if there's one thing of which we're all guilty, it's confusing a good salary with wealth. Having a high income does not guarantee wealth and likewise, a low income does not commit you to a life of poverty. A friend of mine who is a fork-lift driver in a factory has never earned more than the basic wage in his life, yet he owns 47 townhouses and has just bought a jet aircraft. He left school at 15 years of age and continues to work because he loves it. On the other hand I've come across many people who earn six-figure incomes annually and who can't afford to stop working, because they've failed to direct enough income into building wealth. If they did retire, their lifestyle would be drastically affected because they couldn't afford to maintain their luxuries on the income from diminutive or non-existent investments.

Many of today's wealthiest individuals were yesterday's lower income earners, mostly because they planned to do something about increasing their wealth. It's not how much you earn that matters, but rather, what you do with the money you get. Let's get rid of these misconceptions that wealth is measured by how good you look or how much you earn.

Wealth is synonymous with, and is measured by, net worth!

Your net worth is more important than either looks or income. Just consider for a moment... What is your net worth? Add up the value of everything you own, and subtract all that you owe. That's your net worth. It's the total of all your assets minus your liabilities (debts).

The table on the next page will help you calculate your net worth.

What's Your Net Worth?

Assets	Value	Liabilities	Value	
Own Home		Home Mortgage		↑
Investments		Investment Loans		
Car		Car Loans		
Furniture		Furniture Loans		
Other		Other		
TOTAL	**?**	**TOTAL**	**?**	
Net Worth = Total Assets - Total Liabilities = ????				

But, in a more practical sense, we should think of our wealth as something that can provide an income for us when we retire. So you should subtract from this figure the value of your house, car, furniture and other personal items to find out what your real nest egg is worth. After all, what else could you live on if you stopped working today? Would you gamble on Lotto? Would you count on a family inheritance? Or would you rely on charity (usually social security)? Now the chances of winning Lotto are minute, and not all of us are related to the Guinness family. So when you retire, you must have accumulated enough assets, over and above your home and personal belongings, so that this "extra" wealth can produce the income you desire.

While most people acknowledge that their own home forms the bulk of their net worth, they fail to recognise that investment property can be a vehicle for creating this "extra" wealth. Andrew Carnegie said:

"Ninety percent of the world's millionaires became so through owning real estate."

Although property is a time-honoured way of building wealth, it is often overlooked in this technological society that seems to espouse the idea that building wealth, like everything else, must be sophisticated and high-tech. As a result, the last decade has seen a proliferation of packaged "off-the-shelf" investment products. But real estate is just what it says – real property. We can touch it and see it. We walk on it, work in it and live in it. Property is not only the basis of all society, but the basis of all wealth. So if you want to build wealth, if you want to increase your net worth, if you want to be financially independent, you must understand the basic principles of building wealth through property. Walter Lippmann describes property as:

"The only dependable foundation of personal liberty. The original source of freedom."

How to become Wealthy

Have you ever wondered why the rich seem to get richer and the poor seem to get poorer? It's simply because the poor "invest" their money, usually borrowed, into things that make them feel wealthy – cars, boats, clothes and kitchen gadgets that inevitably decrease in value. The rich, however, invest their money, again usually borrowed, into those things that increase in value – such as property. But how do you build wealth through property? What's the game plan? And when do you get to enjoy it all? Firstly, let's look at the figure on the next page to see what most people do with their finances, and then we'll look at what *you* can do.

Most young people spend money as fast as they earn it, so that when they want to buy their first home, they only have a small deposit. As a result, they have to borrow such a large amount, that they struggle for years to repay it in dribs and drabs. Maybe they have some money left over to put towards a small superannuation payout, but what have they got to look forward to at the end of the day? The pension?

But what about you? You can be different. You can look forward to an early retirement and total financial independence and if you've already got some equity in your own home, you're well on your way. Using your own home as a base, you can borrow against the equity to buy a rental property, and then another property and then another.... And so it goes on and on.

While you work, you continue to buy rental properties until you decide that enough is enough and you retire. Then you can sell a property or two to clear your debts, and live off the rents from your remaining rental properties. In time you might sell another property to have an overseas trip or buy a new car – the choice is yours.

For those of you who have scraped and saved all these years to make a dent in your first mortgage, you'll be thinking – why should I go back into debt? But what you should know is that borrowing to buy the next property as an investment is much easier. Why? Because the debt on this next rental property is paid for by two other people – not just you. The tenant and the taxman help pay your interest bill and you are left to pay the remainder. And, it can cost you less than $100 per week to get started. That's why borrowing to buy investment is so much easier than borrowing to buy your own home where YOU pay the lot.

Borrowing to buy investment property, in particular income-producing residential property, is the key to building wealth and it can be achieved on a very average income. You will discover throughout this book just *why* property is the best vehicle for building wealth.

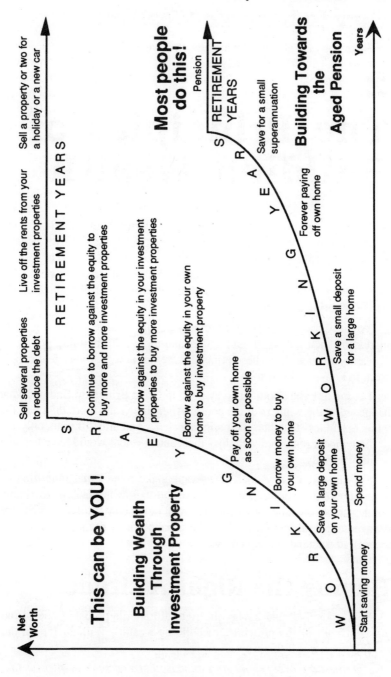

Net Worth

RETIREMENT YEARS

Sell several properties to reduce the debt

Live off the rents from your investment properties

Sell a property or two for a holiday or a new car

This can be YOU!

Building Wealth Through Investment Property

S — Continue to borrow against the equity to buy more and more investment properties

R

A — Borrow against the equity in your investment properties to buy more investment properties

E

Y — Borrow against the equity in your own home to buy investment property

G — Pay off your own home as soon as possible

N

I — Borrow money to buy your own home

K

R — Save a large deposit on your own home

O

W — Start saving money

Most people do this!

Pension

RETIREMENT YEARS

S — Save for a small superannuation

R

A

Y

E

Y

G — Forever paying off own home

N

O

W — Save a small deposit for a large home

Spend money

Building Towards the Aged Pension

Years

2
The Principles of Building Wealth

If wealth can provide for you all the wonderful things you desire, you might well ask, "Why is it that only 1% of the population ever achieve true wealth, while the remaining 99% are content to dream?" The truth is, that in their own small way, most people desire and strive for riches, but they usually opt for the easy way out and gamble on all the schemes that purport to bring quick riches.

Wealthy people are simply ordinary people who do something about increasing their net worth and understand the wealth building principles necessary to succeed. These principles are not new, but very few people seem to know about them.

Let me tell you about a survey done in Great Britain, to find out what happened to the winners of the pools. After five years, more than half the winners had less than half their winnings left. And after 10 years only 1% of the winners remained wealthy - that same 1% that would have become wealthy anyway.

So you see, money does not always make money and inheriting or winning money is not a guaranteed passport to wealth. Unless you know the principles of building wealth, you will never stay wealthy. What are these wealth building principles? Let's have a look at them so that you too will understand the basis of wealth.

Having the Right Attitude

Being positive, and having the right attitude, is probably one of the most difficult of the principles of building wealth. William James, the psychologist, put it this way:

"The greatest discovery of my generation is, that a person can alter his life, by altering his attitude of mind."

Economists are finally beginning to realise that people's attitudes play an extremely important part in the country's economy. It doesn't matter how well you understand the principles of success, you will never become wealthy unless you possess that little bit of something extra – confidence. The following formula is my measure of the state of the economy.

$$E = MC^2$$

where   E   =   Economy

           M   =   Mass of variables including imports, All Ords Index, exports, interest rates, Gross National Product, unemployment etc

and **C = Confidence**

Some of the larger institutions have only just introduced a "confidence indicator", which they now recognise as more important than any other facts and figures that the statisticians can produce. At a national level, if confidence is now considered such an important factor in the economy, think what confidence can do for you on a personal level.

How you think and feel can influence your confidence levels to such an extent that it affects what you do. It's simply a case of – wrong attitude – no confidence – no action – no wealth. Positive thinking can enhance all aspects of our daily lives – including the way we think about wealth and success. Thinking positively means overcoming all obstacles that get, or rather "appear to get" in our way. In his wonderful book "Think and Grow Rich", Napoleon Hill describes some of these obstacles. Here are just a few of the countless "alibis for failure" he lists:

"If I had a good education; If I could get a job; If I had good health; If I did not fear what 'they' would say; If I could save some money; If I only had time; If I could just get a break; If my family were not so extravagant."

The list is endless and you can see how easy it is to find an excuse, or "alibi", for not doing anything at all, or deferring it until tomorrow. As the old Spanish proverb says:

"Tomorrow is often the busiest day of the week!"

To become wealthy you must learn to see the positive attributes of a seemingly bad situation. Don't allow negative thoughts to undermine all your well-intentioned plans. If you listen to the negative people around you, you'll become one of them – one of the 99% of the population who don't achieve the wealth they're capable of.

Taking Responsibility

All too often we put the responsibility for our well-being in the hands of other people and then blame them when things go wrong. Shifting the responsibility for our woes seems to appease our conscience, but it rarely solves our problems. It's the government's fault that I'm unemployed or it's the children's fault that I'm overweight and it's society's fault that I committed a crime. Even in the courts of law, we have a terminology called "diminished responsibility". What this really means is that you can't be blamed because you weren't responsible. There are many people who not only blame others for their problems but they expect others to solve their problems for them. They want someone else to make their decisions for them, to help them lose weight, or to support them in old age. After abusing our bodies for 40 years with fatty foods, alcohol, and cigarettes, we expect doctors to find a miracle cure for our ills.

In Australia, there is a tremendous expectation that the political power of the day will solve all our economic woes. However, it's interesting that Italy has had more than fifty governments since World War Two, and most of the population have no idea who these rotating politicians are! Yet it has a thriving economy, and has largely been unaffected by the world wide slowing in economies. It is more than apparent that Italians have long since accepted that the government cannot be totally responsible for the successful running of the country.

And so too with our finances. We prefer to leave our financial well-being to Lady luck, and if that doesn't work, we leave the responsibility to the government. We condemn the politicians in government for the state of the economy, but fail to realise that the cause of our personal woes has been our own poor attitude. "She'll be right mate" is the catchcry of the nation, but "she" won't be right unless you make it right.

It has been said that people generally fall into three categories: those who make things happen, those who watch things happen and those who wonder what happened. Taking responsibility means you, and you alone have to make it happen. But don't simply *decide* to do it – *do* it.

One afternoon after school, my nine year old son came up to me and asked me this question. "If there are three frogs on a lily pad, and two decide to jump, how many are left?" Thinking deeply, I replied "one". "Wrong" he said gleefully. "Three – they only decided to jump – they haven't jumped yet."

Don't be like a frog on a lily pad and simply decide – once you decide to accept responsibility to do something about increasing your wealth, you have to take the next step and do it.

Setting Goals

Have you made out a will? Most people take the trouble to put pen to paper and set down exactly how they are going to distribute their assets when they die. But very few people bother to set down their wealth goals. We take more time to plan what we're going to do with our money when we're dead, than when we're alive. It pays to *plan* if you really want to be totally financially independent. The mind is a powerful force and goals *can* become a reality once you decide what they are. If you always set out with a specific end in mind, your goal will more than likely be achieved. Most people live up to their expectations; so if you expect nothing, you'll more than likely get nothing.

A social worker in the United States once asked a young man standing in a dole queue, what it was he expected to do with his life. He said that his father was on the dole for his whole life, his grandfather was on the dole for a lifetime, so more than likely he too would spend the rest of his life on the dole. It's sad to think that a negative expectation is usually fulfilled, simply because it's expected.

Achieving your desired level of wealth is a bit like running a personal best time in a race. You may not win the race, but by running your very best, you achieve almost as much satisfaction as the winner. And so too with investing. You don't have to be the richest person in the land, and you may be happy to become financially independent without becoming a millionaire. But no matter what your goal, at least have one.

It's common to hear people, both young and old, say they are going to start saving tomorrow. There's always a reason they can't start today – we're having a baby next month, our little Johnny starts high school next year, we need a new car first, or in the case of teenagers, I'll just buy one more record first. Don't let any obstacles get in your way. As my mother often said to me – "where there's a will, there's a way". On the counter of my local bank, there is a plaque enscribed with a quotation from Vincent T. Lombardi that reads:

"The difference between a successful person and others is not a lack of strength, nor a lack of knowledge, but rather a lack of will."

I often wonder how many people standing in the queue at the bank, take any notice of this little gem. Setting goals is a start, but you need the willpower to see it through. However, the journey towards that goal must not be to the exclusion of everything else. There's not much point in becoming wealthy if you have lost most of your friends, family and sanity somewhere along the way. Set your own financial goals, but keep the rest of your life in perspective and enjoy the journey.

Understanding Rate & Time

One of the most important principles of building wealth is the use of rate and time. It takes time to build real wealth and your thinking needs to expand beyond the time frame of one Christmas to the next if you want to achieve secure wealth. I'm sure everyone has used the old adage that something or other breeds as quickly as rabbits. This is because we have all observed that a pair of rabbits produces several more rabbits, each of which produces more rabbits and so on and so on. And before you know it, there are millions of them. If only we thought of money breeding in the same way – and it can – if only you give it time.

The rate at which an item increases in value can be estimated using the Rule of 72, which effectively states that:

"The number of years it takes an item to double in value multiplied by the growth, is approximately equal to 72."

RULE of 72

		Growth Rate (%)		Years to Double in Value
72	=	3	x	24
72	=	6	x	12
72	≈	7	x	10
72	=	8	x	9
72	=	9	x	8
72	≈	10	x	7
72	=	24	x	3
72	=	36	x	2

From the above table, you can calculate that, if a pie costs $1.50 today and inflation runs at 8%, then the pie would double in value to cost $3.00 in 9 years time (because 8 times 9 is 72). And if property increased in value at around 10% per year, then property prices would double around every 7 years (because 10 times 7 is roughly 72). No matter whether you are talking about pies or property, the Rule of 72 can be used to determine just how quickly the price increases with time. The higher the growth rate, the sooner something will double in value, and the longer the time, the larger the multiplier effect. For property increasing at 10% to 11% per year, this means twice the value in seven years, four times the value in fourteen years, eight times the value in twenty one years, etc etc etc.

Using Debt Wisely

Most people fear debt because parents and other well meaning family members tell you to pay cash for *everything*. While there is an element of truth in this, it should not be taken as a blanket statement that all debt is bad. Debt for consumables can destroy wealth – debt for asset building can build wealth. Let's consider two people who each can spare $4,000 a year. Bill Poor can't wait to get behind the wheel of a brand new $20,000 sports car that is going to cost him $4,000 a year over 10 years. Richie Cash decides that with his $4,000 a year, he can buy a rental property valued at $100,000. Why should a $20,000 car and a $100,000 property cost the same amount – $4,000 a year? Let's look at the two situations.

Bill Poor got a great deal from his local bank and borrowed the entire $20,000, with a principal and interest loan at 14% reducing interest. At $4,000 a year for 10 years, he will clear the loan and own the car outright. However, in the first year, the $4,000 is made up of $3,000 interest and $1,000 principal. Richie Cash borrows $104,500 ($100,000 property price and $4,500 costs) at 14% interest-only. His interest payments are approximately $15,000 a year, with no payment towards the principal, and after 10 years, he still owes $104,500. However, Richie pays only $4,000 of his $15,000 interest bill – net rent is $6,000 ($8,000 rent less $2,000 expenses); he will get a tax refund of about $5,000 each year (because of negative gearing as explained later) and he is left to pay the remaining $4,000. The table below shows you what happens over 10 years.

The Way to Wealth – Car or Property?

CAR ($) – 11% Deprec.			YR	PROPERTY ($) – 11% Apprec.		
Value	Debt	Equity		Value	Debt	Equity
20,000	20,000	0	0	100,000	104,500	-4,500
17,800	19,012	-1,212	1	111,000	104,500	6,500
15,842	17,876	-2,034	2	123,210	104,500	18,710
14,099	16,571	-2,472	3	136,763	104,500	32,263
12,548	15,070	-2,522	4	151,807	104,500	47,307
11,168	13,346	-2,178	5	168,506	104,500	64,006
9,940	11,364	-1,424	6	187,041	104,500	82,541
8,846	9,086	-240	7	207,616	104,500	103,116
7,873	6,468	1,405	8	230,454	104,500	125,954
7,007	3,459	3,548	9	255,804	104,500	151,304
6,236	0	**6,236**	10	283,942	104,500	**179,442**

After 10 Years, at 11% depreciation per year, Bill's car would be worth $6,236. Although he doesn't owe anything on the loan at the end of the term, if he had sold the car at any time up to the seventh year, he would have been going backwards – for most of the time, he owed more than the car was worth. However, at 11% capital growth (appreciation) per year compound, Richie's house would be worth $283,942. Now he still owes the original $104,500, but this gives him an equity of $179,442!! And by that stage, the rent would be greater than the interest payments!!

Let's go one step further. After 10 years, Bill Poor is left with an almost worthless car. To buy another new car, he would need to borrow $50,000, because by then, that's what a new car would cost with inflation. On the other hand, Richie Cash, if he wants to, can sell his property, pay the selling costs, and then pay cash for a brand new car. He'd also have enough to buy one for his wife, one for his son and to go on a holiday!

Which Path Would YOU Choose?

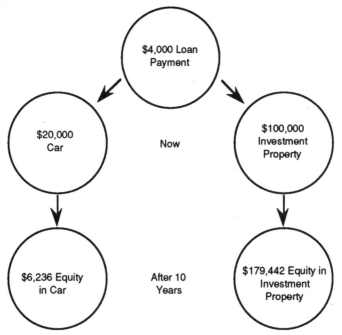

When you next think of debt, think of the following conversation between two young boys.

1st boy: "We are so poor that my Dad owes the bank $2,000."

2nd boy: "We are so rich that my Dad owes the bank $2,000,000."

Gaining Knowledge

"The man who is too old to learn was probably always too old to learn."

Henry Haskins

Knowledge takes the worry out of investing. Knowledge gives you confidence and arms you with sufficient information to evaluate rationally each step in your wealth building plan. We've learned over many years, sometimes the hard way, that knowledge maximises gains and minimises risks. Ultimately, you must become your own expert. But to become an expert, you need to acquire knowledge and you will only accomplish this if you have a real desire to learn.

When I was teaching, it was more than evident that students needed a reason to learn and study. Classes progressed with the usual amount of disruption and disinterest, until that magic word "exam" was mentioned. The transformation was nothing short of miraculous. Students suddenly discovered an overwhelming desire to learn because they had found a very good reason.

Do you have a burning desire to discover the principles of building wealth? What's your attitude to learning? How many books have you bought in the last year to help you make some decisions? Who have you talked to about your wealth building goals and ideas? Have you actively sought the information, or are you going to sit and wait for it to come to you? You may be waiting a long time if this is your attitude.

The fact that most people do not become financially literate until they are adults, and sometimes older adults at that, is a sad reflection on our education system. I for one did not become financially aware until I was in my thirties, even though I completed a University education 10 years earlier.

As a teacher, it was painfully obvious to me that courses in financial management were just not available to most students. Subjects such as "Financial Maths" tended to be part of "General Maths" courses that were directed at the non-achievers. The more academic students often completed a high school education knowing little about interest rates and even less about assets and liabilities. How can we expect them to manage their finances? Presently, the education system emphasises how to acquire the skills to earn money, but ignores the skills involved in managing the money when you get it.

If this emphasis was better balanced, we might not need to spend so much money on saving people from their self-inflicted financial crises. Nevertheless, despite the inadequacies of our present education system, it *is* possible to learn how to become wealthy, no matter how old you are.

When you have armed yourself with sufficient knowledge to understand how to build wealth, you have to take action. But what are the options? When it comes to investing, you really have only four basic choices – cash, shares, property and commodities.

History shows that 90% of people who entered the commodities market in the last decade lost money. If you don't want to be one of those losers, then you must choose from the other three available options – cash, shares or property.

Many investment advisors emphasise the need to diversify and have investments in all three areas. I am more inclined to the advice of Mark Twain who said:

"Put all your eggs in one basket – and watch that basket."

I like to put all my eggs in one basket, the right basket, where I can watch over them very closely and ensure that none break. Putting your eggs into many baskets is simply a form of insurance, so that when a few break, you still have others. It's a bit like having a bet on all the horses in the race. You're pretty well assured of a winner, but at what expense? You've put so much of your money on the losers, that even if the winner pays well, you'll be way behind.

And it's the same with investing. Knowledge gives you the confidence to put all of your money on the winner. My basket is full of residential rental properties. Why is it that I have selected property, and in particular residential property, as my vehicle for building wealth? What it is that makes property the perfect foundation for increasing your net worth, and are there really any alternatives that measure up?

Over the ensuing chapters, I'll illustrate the various attributes of other investments, and demonstrate to you why residential investment property can outstrip the returns from all other investments. These chapters will give you the knowledge that you will need to build wealth through investment property.

PART II

Laying the Foundations of Wealth

3
Wealth from Residential Property

If two of the most important attributes of a good investment are high capital growth and a secure income indexed for inflation, then residential investment property must be the key to building wealth. It has a first class track record of producing high and consistent capital growth, which has typically averaged about 11% compound per year for decades. Not only is the growth itself important, but all evidence suggests that it has performed at 2% to 3% above inflation. Rents, too have more than kept pace with inflation. And so, residential property, with its combination of excellent capital growth and rental income, offers one of the surest and safest means of acquiring riches and building net worth.

But can we expect these trends to continue in the future? To answer this, we must first look at the factors that cause property to increase in value. We should also look to see how general these growth trends have been in a geographical context, and whether cyclic events might have any impact. With this knowledge, you should then at least have an insight into what is possible in the future, and hopefully understand the difference between long-term trends and short-term cycles.

Reasons for Capital Growth

To appreciate why property increases in value, we need to look at the underlying reasons for capital growth. Firstly, there is inflation acting on the costs of land development and the replacement costs of the building. Land scarcity is also a factor because of simple supply and demand, and finally, value can be added by renovations to the building or rezoning of the land as cities spread. Let's take a closer look at each of these factors.

Inflation

Inflation has been around since time immemorial and is not likely to go away in a hurry. It was said that the people from the ancient Chinese Dynasties complained about inflation and that the Roman Empire also experienced rampant inflation. The cost of building materials, labour, and other associated housing costs continually rise with inflation and these costs directly affect land development, building prices and subsequently property values. A quick glance at the table below should dispel any myth that inflation suddenly appeared in the 1980's; it also suggests that on past performances, there is little hope of the current low inflation continuing forever.

Inflation at Work

(Average Annual Compound Rates of Increase)

Range	CPI	Building Materials	Male Av.Wage	Property Growth
1960–1990	8.0%	(n.a.)	9.7%	11.0%
1967–1990	9.3%	9.7%	10.2%	12.1%

The information in this table is based on data supplied by
BIS Shrapnel and the ABS (Australian Bureau of Statistics).

Over the last thirty years, growth in the Consumer Price Index (CPI) has averaged 8% annually. Even during the fifties, when many people suggested there was no inflation, the information from the Australian Bureau of Statistics (ABS) reveals that for the decade from 1948 to 1958, inflation averaged 6.7%!!

Wages have increased faster than inflation over the last thirty years, showing an annual average compound increase of 9.7%. Many people are prepared to swear that they have never had a wage increase and yet a quick glance at the table on the next page would suggest otherwise! Those short-term memories are at work again and it's not until you look at the "big picture" that you begin to appreciate just how much wages have increased. If we look at the 50-year picture, the all-male average weekly wage has risen from a mere $11.20 in 1942 to a staggering $578.20 in 1990. This represents an annual average increase of 8.5% over almost 50 years!   At that rate, by the year 2010, male average weekly earnings will be about $3,000 – or more than $150,000 per year!!

William Vaughan summed up inflation when he described it as:

"Seeing a youngster get his first job at a salary you dreamed of as the culmination of your career."

Average Male Weekly Earnings 1942–1990

Year	Wage ($)	Year	Wage ($)
1942	11.2	1967	67.1
1943	12.8	1968	72.5
1944	13.4	1969	79.0
1945	13.1	1970	86.3
1946	13.0	1971	96.5
1947	13.4	1972	104.4
1948	15.1	1973	120.4
1949	17.7	1974	154.4
1950	19.4	1975	175.7
1951	23.2	1976	195.4
1952	28.4	1977	212.5
1953	31.0	1978	228.2
1954	32.7	1979	248.9
1955	34.3	1980	289.7
1956	36.7	1981	299.4
1957	38.4	1982	341.5
1958	39.5	1983	366.2
1959	43.9	1984	389.5
1960	47.9	1985	413.9
1961	49.3	1986	446.3
1962	50.0	1987	470.0
1963	54.3	1988	505.2
1964	57.7	1989	540.0
1965	59.8	1990	578.2
1966	63.3	***2010**	**3,000.0**

(Information supplied by ABS using several data series)

* Author's projection based on the 50-year trend.

It's interesting that at all my seminars, someone can always tell me what the weekly average earnings were 50 years ago, but no one comes even close to guessing what they would be in just 20 years time if wages continue growing at the same rate!

Land Scarcity

"They're not making any more land."

Will Rogers

It's so easy, in our technological world, to manufacture more and more goods such as microwaves TV's and computers, but no matter how clever we are, we cannot produce more land.

Land scarcity is one of the driving forces behind capital growth. Land which overlooks Sydney Harbour is limited, as is the land around a railway station. Simply through supply and demand, such land increases in value at a faster rate than land that's either less desirable or more plentiful. As populations grow and cities and towns increase in size, suburban sprawl gradually envelopes land around the outskirts, and transforms it into better located property with limited availability. With Australia's population growth, as shown in the figure below, this trend is likely to continue.

Australia's Population Growth

Census Year	Population
1947	7,579,000
1954	8,987,000
1961	10,508,000
1966	11,551,000
1971	13,067,000
1976	14,033,000
1981	14,923,000
1986	16,018,000
1991	*17,000,000
1995	*18,500,000

Data Source: ABS. * Estimated population

Adding Value

Rezoning the land or renovating the buildings has the potential to add value to property. Rezoning usually involves upgrading land to a higher use. For example, rural land rezoned for units should increase in value, as this allows a higher housing density. Renovations in the form of building improvements usually increase property values. Most of us at some time or other have painted a house, renovated a kitchen, or replaced the carpet, all of which may improve the property and increase the prospect of capital growth. Landscaping is an easy method of increasing property values.

Capital Growth – A Profile

Overall, the combination of inflation, land scarcity and value adding have meant that in the past, property values have risen faster than inflation – in fact, between 2% and 3% above inflation.

Let's look at the Australian scene over the past few decades to get a profile of the recent history of capital growth. The data for Sydney and Melbourne (shown on the following two pages) have been obtained from BIS Shrapnel Pty Ltd, Australia's leading economic forecasters. The long-term average annual growth trend in Melbourne has been 11.2% and for Sydney, 10.8%. At these rates, by the year 2010, the estimated median value of property in those cities will be more than a million dollars!!

It is very important to note that the data set on capital growth relates to median priced residential property – which happens to be the most suitable for investment. (The median price is such that half the sales are for less and half are for more.) Median priced property is generally in the lower quarter of the market, and as a result, million-dollar luxury homes, which are susceptible to the vagaries of the economy, do not distort the figures. Although these upmarket properties probably experience around 10% to 11% capital growth over the longer term, their volatility makes this top end of the market the least suitable as investment property and timing is most important. Also, with these properties, rents are not commensurate with property values. However, from the graphs, it's easy to see that timing is not of critical importance for the median priced properties because of the way the "actual values line" weaves around the "trend line".

When you look at these tables and graphs, you can see the dramatic effect of compound capital growth over time. We have seen it happen in the past, but we find it hard to believe it will continue to happen in the future. Will real estate values keep rising? Perhaps I can answer this by relating to you an incident that recently happened to me.

I was talking to a wonderful neighbour of mine about the possibility of rain (Brisbane had just passed through a record 65 days without rain). I commented that I was hurrying to finish the mowing because it looked like rain. He replied "It *will* rain", and I immediately thought he must have heard a weather forecast, and then he added "but I don't know when – could be next year – but it always has, and it always will." This little wisgem, coming from an ex-farmer in his mid-eighties, says more about the course of history and the direction of the future than anything else.

And as for property, historically, values have always risen. And I have no reason to think that they will do anything else but continue to move ahead of inflation and provide a sound basis for building wealth.

Melbourne Median House Values 1960 – 1990

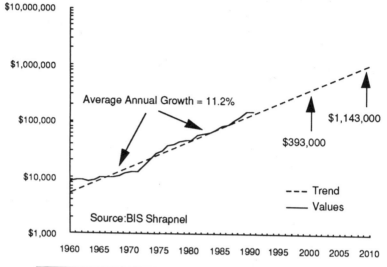

Year	Median Value	Year	Median Value
1960	$8,300	1976	$35,600
1961	$8,700	1977	$38,600
1962	$8,500	1978	$41,300
1963	$8,100	1979	$45,000
1964	$8,800	1980	$44,800
1965	$9,400	1981	$55,600
1966	$9,700	1982	$57,600
1967	$9,400	1983	$59,400
1968	$10,500	1984	$69,300
1969	$11,400	1985	$80,200
1970	$11,800	1986	$85,500
1971	$12,100	1987	$97,000
1972	$14,500	1988	$120,000
1973	$19,800	1989	$151,000
1974	$25,800	1990	$150,000
1975	$27,800	#2010	$1,143,000

Projection Based on continued 11.2% Annual Capital Growth
Source: BIS Shrapnel

Sydney Median House Values 1960 – 1990

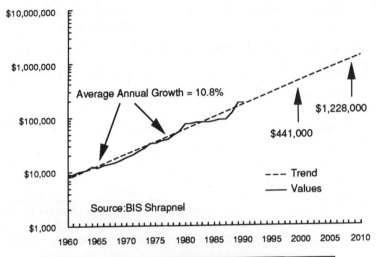

Year	Median Value	Year	Median Value
1960	$8,500	1976	$37,300
1961	$8,800	1977	$39,400
1962	$10,000	1978	$45,800
1963	$10,500	1979	$54,800
1964	$11,900	1980	$74,000
1965	$11,800	1981	$75,800
1966	$12,600	1982	$78,500
1967	$13,400	1983	$79,200
1968	$14,800	1984	$79,400
1969	$16,200	1985	$85,200
1970	$18,500	1986	$90,600
1971	$20,600	1987	$92,100
1972	$23,700	1988	$117,600
1973	$26,400	1989	$183,000
1974	$33,000	1990	$180,000
1975	$33,800	#2010	$1,228,000

\# Projection Based on continued 10.8% Annual Capital Growth
Source: BIS Shrapnel

Figures from various other sources suggest that these long-term trends in capital growth are the same for other capital cities as well as the larger regional cities. The figures below are average annual growth figures for the last decade (1980 – 1990), during which time the CPI averaged 8.1%.

Average Annual Capital Growth (1980 – 1990)

Capital City	Growth	Regional City	Growth
• Sydney	12.8%	* Geelong	12.5%
• Melbourne	12.7%	* Bendigo	11.2%
• Brisbane	11.2%	* Ballarat	11.4%
• Adelaide	10.8%	+ Townsville	11.5%
• Perth	9.8%	+ Cairns	13.9%
• Canberra	11.6%	+ Bundaberg	10.4%

Source: • Real Estate Institute of Australia, Market Facts (Median Values)
*   * Valuer General's Department, Victoria (Median Values)
\+   + Lands Dept and Real Estate Institute of Qld (Average Values)

Other western countries have experienced similar patterns of property growth. In the United Kingdom, the records from the Domesday Book of 1068 show that capital growth has averaged almost 10% for more than 900 years. In the United States, the average long-term growth trend from 1968 to 1990 was 8.0% (see chart below), while inflation over the same period averaged 5.9%.

Median Sales Price of Existing Single–Family Homes in the United States (1968 – 1990)

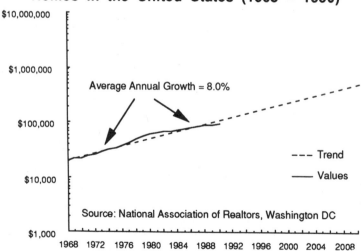

A typical comment I often hear about property in the forties and fifties is that "If a house in 1950 was worth $5,000, and three years later is worth $7,000, then it's *just* $2,000 more – capital growth must have been lower way back then!" However, it is misleading to compare absolute values.

A few thousand dollars may seem like peanuts to us now, but in those days it was a lot of money – in fact, it represented an average annual growth of 11%!!! You must look at the percentage increases, not dollar increases. Everything is relative and in years to come, I'm sure we'll look back to today and ponder the fact that property in Australia has risen by a paltry few hundred thousand dollars in just 10 years, when all around us property is valued in the millions.

After sifting through old records and newspapers in libraries, as well as talking to many people who have bought residential property over the years, it was not hard to find a myriad of examples of how property has increased in value. Think back to the properties that you have bought and sold over the years, and use the Rule of 72 to work out their annual capital growth. And remember to look over at least a 10-year time frame. I'll bet you're saying to yourself, "I wished I'd kept that house." Or "I wished I'd bought a few at that price!" Or "I wished I knew then what I know now." Don't let another twenty years go by without doing something about it, or you'll find yourself saying the same things again.

A few of the properties for which I have specific information are listed below. The average annual compound growth rates have been calculated and you should notice that all of these growth rates are more than 9.5%.

Specific Examples of Capital Growth

Property Location	Year Bought	Initial Price ($)	1992 Value ($)	No. of Years	Annual Growth
Capalaba, Qld	1976	23,500	107,000	16	10.0%
Kippa Ring, Qld	1973	13,500	95,000	19	11.8%
Church Pt, NSW	1972	45,000	550,000	20	13.3%
Warriewood, NSW	1968	13,750	350,000	24	14.4%
Gosford, NSW	1967	1,300	150,000	25	20.9%
Seaforth, NSW	1960	11,000	800,000	32	14.3%
Forster, NSW	1959	1,000	35,000	33	11.4%
Margate, Qld	1950	2,000	90,000	42	9.5%
New Farm, Qld	1940	1,300	150,000	52	9.6%
Cleveland, Qld	1915	90	150,000	77	10.1%

Let's look at the last example in more detail. This block of land was advertised for sale in the Redland Mercury for 45 pounds ($90) in 1915. The advertisement read:

"For sale. First class half acre Queen Street, next to Methodist Church. Fenced both sides £45. Apply W. Bennett, Ellis Street, South Brisbane."

We know the value in 1992 was around $150,000, because an identical property close by was sold recently for more than that. This increase in value from $90 in 1915 represents an average compound capital growth of about 10.1% per year over 77 years. (Verify for yourself how $90 can become $150,000 by doubling the $90 every seven years for 77 years.)

Although the growth each year may not have been a constant 10.1%, slow growth in some years would have been compensated for by large jumps in other years. During these 77 years, there have been two world wars, a depression, a few recessions and other economic crises, yet the value of the property has still averaged more than 10% growth per year.

If property values continue to grow at around 10% per annum, then according to the Rule of 72, values should double about every seven years (quadruple in 14 years, eight times their value in 21 years, sixteen times their value in 28 years etc). If we project the value of the $90 block of land into the future at these multiples, the results are staggering.

By the year 2013, at this rate, this block of land should be worth more than a million dollars, and by the year 2020, more than two million dollars!! The table below shows you just how the compounding of rate and time can affect the capital growth of this land worth $90 in 1915.

Capital Growth at Work

Year	Property Value
1915	$90
1992	$150,000
*1999	$300,000
*2006	$600,000
*2013	$1,200,000
*2020	$2,400,000
*2027	$4,800,000
*2034	$9,600,000
*2041	$19,200,000
*2048	$38,400,000

* Projected values based on 10% growth per year

Rental Income – A Profile

Investing in income-producing residential property relies on tenants. But will the supply of tenants continue in the future? Although one of the great Australian dreams is to own one's own home, the figures (shown below) suggest that a reduced percentage of Australians own their home now (66%) compared to a decade ago (73%), and that more and more people are renting property. In fact, approximately one in three residential properties is a rental property!

Increase in Numbers of Tenants

Type of Household	1978		1988	
Owner/Purchaser	(73%)	3,325,000	(66%)	4,095,900
Renter	(24%)	1,093,100	(29%)	1,817,000
– Private		827,300		1,188,500
– Govt		197,800		308,900
– Other		68,000		319,600
Rent Free	(3%)	114,000	(5%)	260,000
Total		4,532,500		6,173,400

Source: Australian Bureau of Statistics

Similar trends have occurred in the United States, where the National Association of Realtors reported (1990) – *Nationally, the home ownership rate dropped from 65.6% of households in 1980 to 63.9% in 1989.*

This trend, together with the continual immigration of people and new household formations, should ensure the need for rental accommodation for many years.

Has rent kept pace with inflation? BIS Shrapnel data indicates that the weighted average for rents over the past 17 years has shown an average annual increase of 9.2%. Data from the Australian Bureau of Statistics (shown on the next page) reveals that over the longer term (1947 – 1986), rents increased at 9.3% per annum, and that the level of rent consistently measured around 15% to 20% of the male average wage.

Another important consideration is the vacancy factor. Information for the capital cities from the Real Estate Institute of Australia over 9 years, indicates this has been as low as 0.7% in Adelaide in 1982, and as high as 7.1% in Perth in 1990. A vacancy factor of about 4% is considered a good balance between supply and demand for rental accommodation. A lower vacancy factor indicates a very tight rental market with tenants "fighting" for the right to rent property.

Average Median Weekly Rent 1947 – 1986

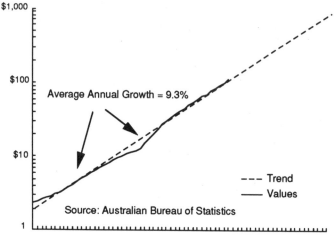

Census* Year	Av. Weekly Median Rent	Male Av. Weekly Wage	Rent as % of Weekly Wage
1947	$2.4	$13.4	17.9%
1954	$3.5	$32.7	10.7%
1961	$6.6	$49.3	13.4%
1966	$9.6	$63.3	15.1%
1971	$13.0	$96.5	13.5%
1976	$27.5	$195.4	14.1%
1981	$45.5	$299.4	15.2%
1986	$71.5	$446.3	16.0%
1991	•$110.0	•$580.0	•18.9%

* Information supplied by the Australian Bureau of Statistics

• Estimate based on information available.

Note: Because the median rents cover such a broad spectrum of housing such as houses, units and furnished flats, and all areas including country as well as city, the rent levels may appear low compared to rents in the capital cities, however the trend is more than evident.

Property Cycles

Although we continually refer to an average compound capital growth of around 10% to 11% per year, it is not constant each and every year. In reality, property values tend to increase in cycles. In some years, growth may be nothing, while in others, it may be as much as 40% or 50%.

You need to understand that the cyclical events are just what the name implies – cyclical. For short-term investors, the timing of these cycles is most important, but for long-term property investors, these fluctuations even out. The diagram below shows you the sequence of events in cycles.

The Economic Cycle

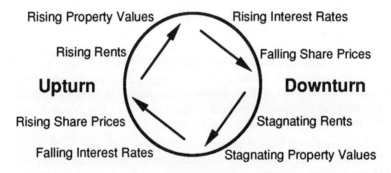

Boom

Rising Property Values   Rising Interest Rates

Rising Rents   Falling Share Prices

Upturn   **Downturn**

Rising Share Prices   Stagnating Rents

Falling Interest Rates   Stagnating Property Values

Bust

Let me describe how cycles affected the value one of our properties in Brisbane. Over a 16 year period between 1976 and 1992, capital growth averaged 10% ($23,500 to $107,000). However, between 1983 and 1987, annual capital growth was only 2.4% ($50,000 to $55,000). But over the next five years, the annual growth averaged 14.2% ($55,000 to $107,000).

The cyclical nature of the property market is very much related to the herd mentality of human nature. Everyone builds when everyone else is building, buys when everyone else is buying, and sells when everyone else is selling. As a classic example of this all-or-nothing mentality, I'd like to summarise what happened to the property market in an area south of Brisbane. These events are typical of most Australian property scenes.

In the mid 1980's, it was very difficult, if not impossible, to find rental accommodation. This situation had arisen because of the abolition of some of the tax benefits of negative gearing and because developers had fled the scene during the preceding years of recession. This resulted in fewer property investors and fewer rental properties. The demand for rental accommodation became enormous. With mounting pressure on the rental market, rents climbed through the roof, rising by an average of 40% ($100 to $140) in about 18 months. (Incidentally, the 1988 World Fair "EXPO" was a convenient scape goat for the resultant rise in rents.)

In late 1987, a rather unusual combination of events followed. The re-introduction of the right to offset negative gearing against other income, the sharemarket crash, the lowering of interest rates, and the high rental yields, together with the already pent-up demand for property, precipitated an onslaught of buyers into the property market. This was immediately followed by substantial increases in property values as demand outstripped supply. The average prices of property in Brisbane increased by more than 50% in just two years taking the median value from $62,000 in 1987 to $93,800 in 1989 (Source: Real Estate Institute of Queensland).

Out of the woodwork came all the property developers who had been "mustering cattle out west". They jumped on the band wagon, developing and building at a tremendous rate. New houses, unit developments and commercial buildings appeared almost overnight. What followed in 1991 was highly predictable. These developers, apparently oblivious to the laws of supply and demand, continued on their merry way. The resultant glut of properties, in particular units and townhouses, was as apparent to Joe Average as it was to the astute property analyst.

There were now more than enough rental properties, and agents were having difficulty renting them. Meantime, developers were left holding the bag – or the properties. The stage was then set for a "bust" and sales by mortgagees in possession followed in quick succession.

The developers began to vacate the scene altogether and no doubt, this will lead to a future shortage of developments. With the inevitable return to prosperous times, tenants will again return to look for rental properties. First-home buyers will be out in force, further reducing the number of properties available for rent – and off we go again. The great South American philosopher George Santayana said:

"The only lesson history teaches man is that it keeps on repeating itself."

You'd think that human beings would learn from experience, but this appears not to be. Human nature drives us to do what everyone else is doing when everyone else is doing it, but those 1% who are going to achieve financial success, must learn to fight against human nature. Buying property when everyone else is not requires confidence, but if horizons are long-term, then short-term humps and bumps are ironed out giving way to sustained capital growth.

4

Comparing Cash, Shares and Property

Just before June 30 one year, a friend told me he had recently bought shares in a pine plantation. When I asked why, he replied that it was now the end of the financial year and he was about to pay "heaps" of tax unless he "did something". A few years later, the pine plantation venture collapsed and my friend was left holding a bundle of worthless shares. He did get his tax deduction for that first year – but at what cost? Was he trying to build wealth, or simply trying to reduce tax?

The vehicle you use for building wealth must satisfy *all* the attributes of a great investment – not just one or two. We have already established that in the long-term, residential property offers excellent capital growth and rental income. But what other considerations are there? You also need to consider tax effectiveness, real return on investment, security, liquidity and the degree of control. How does property fare when all these things are considered and how does it stack up against the alternatives – cash and shares? Let's now examine all the attributes that make property a great platform for building wealth and compare it with the alternatives.

Capital Growth

Good capital growth is fundamental to increasing net worth. We have already seen the power of rate and time in compounding wealth, and why it is important to select an investment with a high rate of capital growth. Remember the Rule of 72?

What about the capital growth of cash? Cash has no capital growth, and consequently it is subject to the ravages of inflation. Do you know of anyone who became wealthy by investing money in the bank? I certainly don't, in fact quite the reverse is true. A deposit of $200,000 in the bank today will be worth one fifth of its value in terms of what it will buy in 20 years time at 8% inflation (the past 30-year trend).

Although you may receive income from money invested in the bank, the capital growth is zero. You saw in chapter 2 that this results in the income losing value over time in real money terms, necessitating a greater income to buy the same goods. We are taught that saving money is good, and so it is, but it should only be a means to an end, not the end itself. You'll need *some* money in a bank to ensure the success of your property investments, but it should not be considered as the vehicle to wealth.

How about shares? Don't they offer high capital growth? It may surprise you that the upward trend of the All Ordinaries Index over the last 100 years has averaged around 5% compound per year (Data Source: The Australian Stock Exchange). To make realistic comparisons with property growth, which has been well documented for the last thirty years (1960 – 1990), the growth trend for the All Ordinaries Index for the same 30 year period was calculated – and found to be just 6.9%!

The graph below reveals the fickleness of the sharemarket highs and lows that rise and fall far above and below this long-term trend. Even many large financial institutions, with their trained investment specialists, rarely pick the highs and lows. How can you, as an individual player, expect to be a better judge?

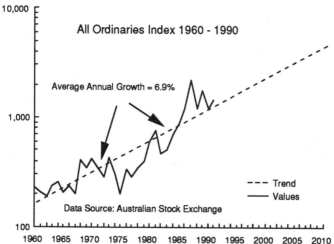

When Is the Right Time to Buy Shares?

All Ordinaries Index 1960 - 1990

Average Annual Growth = 6.9%

Data Source: Australian Stock Exchange

- - - Trend
—— Values

Fortunes *have* been made on the sharemarket, but because of its volatility, you need to be a "when-to" investor. You need to know *when* to buy and *when* to sell. Not only do you need to be a "when-to" investor but you also need to be a "which-to" investor because the performance of individual shares is even more volatile than the All Ordinaries Index. The instant tradability of shares contributes to this volatility. This adds to the excitement of the sharemarket, but it does not necessarily add to your wealth.

Even if you don't speculate on shares and hold long-term, the average growth long-term (as we have seen in the 30-year graph above) is less than 7% – a rate that is lower than inflation (8%) over the same period. Also, the highs and lows can be so severe that even long-term holding may not iron out all the humps and bumps. But property, and in particular residential property in the bottom quarter of the market (median-priced property), is not subject to such wild fluctuations.

There are many companies whose share values have plummeted out of existence creating massive capital losses for their share holders. Although the median price of residential property may stagnate, it rarely plunges and I doubt that there are any residential properties in the major towns and cities that are now "worthless". Also, small investors are powerless to control their own share investments and insider trading is a big concern. A recent newspaper article (Brisbane Sun, May 1991) cited 79 insider trading cases examined by the National Companies and Securities Commission, of which only seven had gone to trial, and no one was convicted. Reasons given for these dismissals were that it was too difficult under current laws to secure convictions, "although there was almost certainly some insider trading going on in Australia".

When it is possible to manipulate the sharemarket artificially, how can *you* as an average investor, expect to win? However, by its sheer size, the property market and especially residential property, cannot be manipulated. The table below gives you an indication of the size of the asset markets in Australia today and demonstrates the magnitude of the residential property market.

Asset Market Values In Australia – 1992

Value	$ Billion
Australian Trading Banks	55
Retail Turnover	73
Retail Property	95
Commercial Property	120
Sharemarket	201
Residential Property	608

Perhaps it is timely to compare the growth trends for the major indices over the last 30 years to determine their effect in multiplying your wealth. From the graph below, it's very easy to see that property growth has outstripped both shares and inflation (CPI) while the All Ordinaries Index growth trend for shares has performed below inflation.

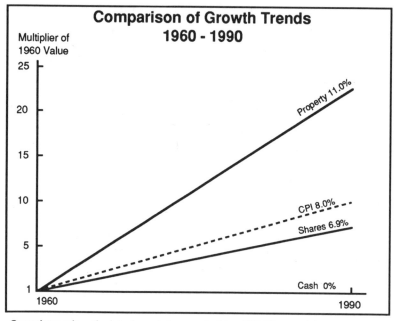

Growth trends calculated on data supplied by: BIS Shrapnel (property), ABS (CPI), Australian Stock Exchange (All Ords Index for shares).

The multiplier could be calculated from the Rule of 72 (refer back to chapter 3) so in effect, property has doubled approximately every six and a half years, the CPI has doubled every nine years while the All Ordinaries Index has doubled only every 10 years. What this means over a 30 year period is that property is now about 23 times its value in 1960, the CPI is about 10 times the 1960 value, but the All Ords Share Index is only 7.5 times it's 1960 value. Cash has no growth and consequently will always have the same value - but less in real terms because of inflation.   The median price of Sydney property in 1960 was about $8,000 and in 1990 was more than 20 times that value at around $180,000. In 1960, the All Ords Index averaged 200 and in 1990 was about 1500, a multiple of 7.5. You should now begin to understand and appreciate why capital growth is such an important factor in building wealth through property

Income

No matter what your investment, it must generate income. Ideally, the income from your investments should be sufficient to replace your normal salary when you retire, and this income should be indexed for inflation. There's not much point in being asset-rich but cash-poor. Income is very important both while you are building wealth and when you finally reap the rewards in your retirement.

This source of income must also have capital growth so that the capital base from which the income is generated continually rises with inflation. Suppose for example that you have a capital base of $100,000 that grows at 11% per annum and produces income of 5% of the capital value. In the first year, the income would be $5,000 (5% of $100,000). But in the following year, when the capital base is $111,000 (increased by 11% growth), the income would be $5,550 (5% of $111,000). So you can see it is not only important to find an investment that generates income, but also one that is indexed to inflation through capital growth.

The regularity with which cash investments provide income is what attracts many people to debentures and term deposits. Cash is an excellent source of direct income, but this income is not inflation-indexed because the underlying capital base does not grow. Therefore any lump sum will provide a seemingly good income initially, but in the longer term, this income will not be able to purchase the same goods that are increasing in value with inflation. Also, interest from cash deposits is fully taxed, so the interest rate you are quoted is not the interest rate you enjoy *after* tax. This means that most of your interest would disappear with the twin ravages of taxation and inflation.

Shares do pay dividends, and dividend imputation can make the income slightly more attractive. It is also possible to gear (borrow money) into shares with additional tax benefits. However, the income from shares can be extremely unpredictable depending on the nature of the company. This makes negative gearing very productive in terms of a healthy tax refund, but can play real havoc with your cash flow predictions. Furthermore, the underlying capital base producing this income, on average, has not kept pace with inflation.

On the other hand, tenanted property should provide a steady source of rental income linked to steady capital growth, not only while you are in the process of building wealth, but also for your retirement. So, providing appropriate steps are taken to ensure low vacancies, residential property can continue to produce a regular source of indexed income, long after you have retired. Isn't this the ultimate aim of your wealth building strategy?

Tax Effectiveness

Taxation erodes investment returns just as surely as inflation. Tax is a fact of life, but rather than wasting precious energy in trying to find ways to "avoid" tax, you should be trying to find ways to maximise your after-tax returns. It's simply a matter of structuring your investments in relation to the tax laws. Let's look at the three areas of investment to see how they are affected by taxation.

Cash investments are not favoured by the tax laws as the interest is taxed at your marginal rate of tax. But people still bury their money in banks and expect to live off the interest for ever more. If the interest rate is 11% and your marginal tax rate is about 40% (38% + 1.25% Medicare), then the real rate of return is only 6.6%. The example below shows you how to calculate the real interest on a $4,000 cash investment.

Tax on Cash

Investment	=	$4,000
Interest on money	=	11%
Income	=	$440
Tax payable	=	$176
Real Income	=	$264
Rate of Return	=	$264 x 100%
		$4,000
	=	6.6%

When inflation of 8% is accounted for, the real return is minus 2.6%!

To encourage share investments in Australian companies, a scheme called "dividend imputation" has been implemented by the government. The scheme gives a tax credit to the shareholder for tax already paid by the company, thereby averting double taxation. This is a much fairer system, but you still must weigh the tax benefit with long-term growth (which we have already shown to be less than 7% on average for the last thirty years). Further tax benefits are possible through negative gearing into shares, but because of the volatility of shares, this is highly risky.

On the other hand, if you negatively gear into investment property, the more consistent capital growth makes this strategy much more secure than for shares. Negative gearing will be dealt with in much greater detail in chapter 16 but it's important to look at just how it does affect property investment. When you borrow money for any reason at all, you must pay interest on the principal borrowed. If it's to buy your own home, then you pay the entire interest bill.

But when you borrow money to invest in rental property, the interest bill is shared between the tenant, the taxman and you. This means that a rental property could cost you less than $100 per week, depending on your marginal rate of tax.

Let's see how this happens. Suppose the property value is $100,000 and to buy it, you borrow $104,500 (including purchasing and borrowing costs amounting to $4,500) at 14% interest, or around $15,000 per year (see chapter 11 to find out how you can borrow the entire purchase price plus all the costs associated with the property).

If you clear $6,000 per year in rent from the tenant ($8,000 rent less $2,000 expenses), and you receive a tax refund of $5,000, then the real cost of the property to you is only $4,000 (or $80 per week). This means that you pay only 27% of the interest bill pie!

Who Pays Your Interest Bill?

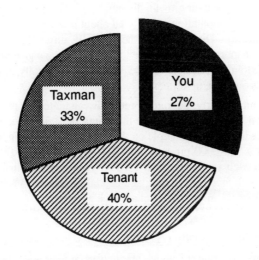

Now of course, these percentages will vary depending on such things as rent, expenses, the interest rate and most importantly, your marginal tax rate. And while it is quite true that negative gearing assists higher-income earners more, I consider property investment to be by far the best wealth building vehicle there is, no matter what level your income. I know many property investors who earn less than $20,000 per year, and are well on their way to achieving total financial independence long before their higher-salaried bosses.

What about the capital gains tax? You'll see in chapter 14 why this tax has minimal effect on long-term property investors.

Return on Investment

How do you measure the real rates of return on your investments and what's the reliability of projecting these rates into the future? Most people think in terms of interest paid by a bank as a yardstick. So they compare interest from a bank, to dividends from shares, to rent from a property. However, this is a gross oversimplification and does not take into account such things as the capital growth and tax implications. The best and most accepted way to calculate the real after-tax returns is to relate the money you outlay over time with what you get at the end.

You saw on the previous page that the after-tax rate of return on money invested in the bank at 11% was really only 6.6%. Not only is it easy to calculate your real after-tax rate of return from invested cash, but it is easy to predict what it will be in the future because all the variables are fixed.

What about shares? It is possible to calculate the after-tax returns on shares by accounting for their growth, dividends, and tax benefits (negative gearing and dividend imputation). But what about predicting returns from shares in the future? Dividends can be a totally unreliable source of income and it is inappropriate to use the long-term average growth (6.9%) because of its extreme volatility. Consequently, it is virtually impossible to predict returns on share investments.

For investment property, the rate of return is calculated by relating the real after-tax cost (outlay or income) to the equity built up in the property (end gain). Let's look at the example on the previous page again, where it was shown that a $100,000 property may cost you around $4,000 in the first year. If, in each successive year for five years, your contribution is reduced in line with increases in rent, and capital growth is 11% per year, then over five years we might have figures such as these.

Year 1	Year 2	Year 3	Year 4	Year 5	Equity
$4,000	$3,500	$3,000	$2,500	$2,000	$64,000

If the property cost you the above amounts each year and equity built up to $64,000 over the five years, then the after-tax rate of return is more than 50%! (i.e. for an account to add up to $64,000 after the five annual "deposits" as above, the interest rate would have had to have been about 50% after-tax). But what about the reliability of predicting these returns in the future? For residential property in the bottom quarter of the market, both the annual capital growth (10 –12%) and rental increases (9.2%) over the last 30 years have been high and consistent (see chapter 3). On this basis, I would expect that these rates of return are more than achievable in the future. (See Appendix for a more detailed description of Property Investment Analysis by Computer.)

Security

There's not much point in channelling your hard-earned money into an investment only to find that it's no longer there when you retire. In a climate where many people have lost their life savings through the collapse of financial institutions, it is of paramount importance to place your funds in a secure investment.

But it is also important to put risk in perspective. After all, life is one big risk. When you have a shower, you run the risk of getting burnt – a minute risk that you have learned to minimise by turning the cold water on first. You don't avoid having a shower just because there is an element of risk involved. You learn to take some precautions. And so it is with investing. No investment is 100% secure – even money in the bank. But if you don't take some risk with your money now, however slight, you run the risk of having to live on social security later in life. Most people defer risk. They put off making a forward step until retirement is just around the corner, and then it's too late. Although we cannot eliminate risk altogether, it's important to choose an investment that is powerful enough to build wealth, but is secure enough for us not to be losing sleep.

How secure are cash deposits? Most people would believe they are reasonably secure. I see nothing secure about money in a bank that is continually eroded by inflation. I know of many people with large sums of money "invested" in the bank and they tell me it makes them feel very secure. Yet they are the first to complain six or seven years down the track when their money won't buy as much as it used to. Is that security? To seek security continually is to ignore opportunity.

What about the security of shares? Banks recognise the highly volatile nature of shares and will generally only accept between 10% and 50% of the face value of shares as a form of security against which money is loaned. Some banks will not even accept shares as a form of security but will readily hold property as the collateral for money borrowed to buy shares. What does that tell you about the security of shares? If the banks cannot be sure of share values at any point in time, how can you be?

In contrast with shares, banks have always recognised the security of property and many banks will accept up to 90% of the property value, in particular residential property, as a form of security (i.e. mortgages). What could be more secure than property when the leading financial institutions hold its security in such high esteem?

Furthermore, to repeat what I said earlier, real estate is just what its name implies – real property. You can touch it, see it, drive past it and *insure* it.

Liquidity

Cash is highly liquid. There's no doubt about that. Even with some term deposits, in mitigating circumstances, your cash can be obtained fairly readily. Although you'll never become wealthy by putting money in the bank, you should always have some cash as a means of supporting your other investments - having *some* cash is better than a sleeping pill!

Shares are also very liquid. This liquidity and spontaneity in obtaining a sale adds to the excitement of playing the sharemarket but it is ironical that this easy liquidity is a major contributing factor to the sharemarket's volatility. A person can respond to good or bad news by buying or selling shares instantaneously – but so can everyone else, creating an immediate supply and demand crisis. It is this spontaneity that attracts the white collar punter to the sharemarket. How appropriate to see an advertisement for the TAB in the midst of the sharemarket columns of a recent edition of a national newspaper. It read:

EASY   MONEY

QUICK   RESULT

GREAT   FUN

It seems that the TAB and sharemarket attract a similar type of person. Unfortunately, because of the highly volatile nature of the sharemarket, timing can be critical when you are liquidating shares. Yes, you can sell when you want, but no, there is no guarantee you'll get your initial capital back, even if you sell many years into the future.

Property is "perceived" to be illiquid. This perceived illiquidity is one of the very things that makes property so much more stable than shares. Usually, when property investors need money, they put their property on the market and then wait several months to finalise the sale and "see" the money. This time-lag has the effect of insulating property from the "buy–sell" mentality that drives the sharemarket to all-time highs and lows. I said "perceived illiquidity", because most investors think that a sale is the only way to extract cash from property.

But one of the greatest attributes of property is its borrowing potential. If you need money in a hurry to visit Grandma in England, you can refinance the property and borrow the money. This not only eliminates the need to sell at short notice, it may eliminate the necessity to sell at all. It is probably advisable to set up some appropriate refinancing measures well before you need it (see chapter 17).

Control

Last but not least, any investment that makes you wealthy, must offer complete personal control. You and you alone must have control over every aspect of your assets. You can decide just what the investment will be in the first place and how it fits into your wealth building plan. This does not mean that you have to do everything yourself. What it does mean is that you have the capacity to delegate to other people those aspects of your investment of which you either have no desire to be part, or no time to complete.

Cash deposits give you control. You have the ability to do what you like with your money – whenever you like. But the great aspect of the control you have over cash, is that its accessibility can give you even greater control over the property you hold.

Shares offer you the least amount of control of all three investments. Unfortunately, when you buy shares you are at the whim and mercy of the directors of the company, and although there are shareholders meetings, voting is usually in proportion to the number of shares you hold. Small investors have very little say in the destiny of a company and control usually lies with the larger institutions. I guess the only positive aspect of handing over control is that if you lose, you can always blame someone else. Is that what you want?

However, direct investment into property gives you complete control over all aspects of your investment. Apart from choosing the location, style and price of your property, you can choose the tenant, the property manager, how your finance is structured, where you borrow the money and what level of debt you desire. *You* decide when (or if) to sell the property. The list is infinite – but more importantly, you can choose your level of involvement. *You* can do as much or as little as you feel like. When you buy investment property, the ultimate control of your wealth building plan lies with you.

5
What about Managed Investments?

Not long ago, in a financial investment book, I saw a chapter headed "Money for a Rainy Day – Superannuation, Trusts, Rollovers, Annuities". I think this sums up what these funds will do for you. Although managed investments are not the greatest wealth generators, for many people these funds will provide their *only* little "nest egg" for them when they retire. These people are the ones who either don't want to, or can't be bothered to look after their own financial security. Yet with a little know-how (which this book should provide), a little money (maybe less than $100 a week), and a little effort, you can attain far greater wealth by taking responsibility for your own financial destiny, and by investing directly in property.

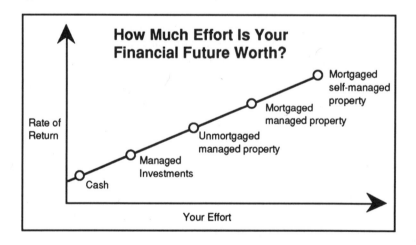

Managed investments are just what they say they are – managed. Someone else takes all the effort out of investing your money for you – but they also take all the cream. There are salesmen's commissions and administration and management fees to be paid from the profits of the managed funds. But ask yourself – "What is the source of these profits?" Fund managers invest your money into the only three investment options available – cash, shares, and property. So it's highly likely that your money will end up in investment properties anyway. However, the returns to you are significantly reduced by all the middlemen between your money and the properties.

Now it's not the purpose of this book to criticise these managed funds, for I recognise their usefulness to many people. But I want to offer you an alternative – one that so few people take - direct investment in property. And one of the aims of this book is to show you how simple, and how much more beneficial it is, to control your own financial destiny through direct investment in residential property. The choice is yours.

> *"Two roads diverged in a wood, and I –*
>
> *I took the one less travelled by*
>
> *And that has made all the difference."*
>
> *Robert Frost*

Direct investment in property can make all the difference to you, too.

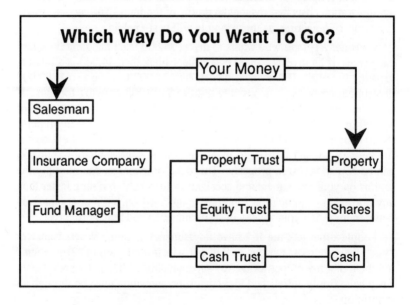

Superannuation

The government wants people to be more responsible for their own retirement and is gradually implementing compulsory superannuation, reducing the need for pensions in the future. However, the purpose of these schemes, with all their limitations, is not to make you wealthy. It is simply to free the government of any responsibility to look after you in your retirement. Now many of you probably already have super. That's OK. But if you want to build real wealth, you must go beyond the confines of normal superannuation. Let's compare normal superannuation to direct investment in rental property.

In superannuation, you can only accrue about seven times your final average salary before the tax benefits run out. So, if you earn $30,000 a year, you'll be limited to about $200,000. And you've seen how quickly this disappears! You can accumulate more, *if* you take half as a pension. But there is no limit to the amount of property you can accumulate.

Tax deductions for super have improved recently, but are still limited. You cannot claim the full contribution, and in many cases, such as for an employer-sponsored scheme, you cannot claim anything. On the other hand, the deductions available for investment property are unlimited.

The rate of return from superannuation compared to income-producing investment property is much lower for several reasons. Firstly, there are administration costs that reduce the profits of the fund. The second reason has to do with gearing, as this example will best explain.

Consider a person who wants to invest $4,000 from his $35,000 salary each year. If he invests $4,000 into a super fund, then $4,000 is all that is growing in value. However, if it costs him $4,000 to get into a $100,000 investment property, it is possible to have $100,000 growing for him. If both the super fund and property grow at 11%, it's easy to see that 11% of $4,000 in a super fund is a lot less than the 11% of $100,000 in property ($440 compared to $11,000). Why is there such a difference? Leverage is the key. You can't borrow to invest in normal superannuation, but you can borrow to invest in property. This debt, or leverage, can multiply the returns on your investment and accelerate your wealth building faster than any normal superannuation fund (see chapter 10 for a direct comparison between investing your money in superannuation and rental property).

People often ask me if I have any superannuation. When I answer "yes", they are most curious to find out which fund I am in. But when I tell them that my properties are my superannuation, they don't understand. They have firmly entrenched ideas that superannuation must be through an institution.

Just ponder for a moment or two. What do you expect from normal superannuation? You want it to give you long-term security and some income on your retirement. Don't you? Doesn't investment in rental property accomplish all of this and more? Doesn't property give you long-term security and income for your retirement in the form of rent? And don't you pay into it year after year by paying some of the interest bill? Then in effect, it's a form of superannuation – yet a far more powerful and more flexible form of superannuation. It just takes a little rearrangement of our thoughts, and a little lateral vision, to think of it that way.

Property Trusts & Syndicates

Since this book is about investment property, it seems appropriate to look at two special types of managed funds that involve property – namely property trusts and property syndicates.

When you buy into a property trust, you become a beneficiary of the trust without "owning" the building. You can buy into and out of the trust at your whim, so long as there are no moratoriums. Property trusts may be "listed", whereby their units can be traded on the stock exchange through brokers at the listed price, which is subject to market fluctuations. If they are "unlisted", they can be bought and sold by the trust directly at "nominated valuation" prices. Property trusts in general, do not have a good track record. However, in the midst of all the adverse publicity, a few property trusts have not only survived, but have done extremely well. It is noteworthy that some of the better performing trusts have specialised in residential property. Nevertheless, it is extremely difficult to separate the wheat from the chaff and determine which of these trusts are solid.

In a property syndicate, you become a part owner in a specific building. Usually the only way out is to wait until the syndicate terminates and the building is sold, although some syndicates do make provision for selling at the discretion of the manager. Usually, property syndicates consist of a small consortium of investors (about 20) with a selected fund manager and property manager. Each syndicate is established to purchase a specific property, and because of the minimum of overheads and middlemen, these syndicates can be quite profitable, particularly since they can be geared to a high level. One of the more successful syndicate operations in the past, managed by D.F. Johnson (see the reading list in chapter 20), mostly bought residential properties.

Property trusts and syndicates have a limited use as a compromise for someone who is interested in property investment, but does not want to commit themselves to outright ownership.

6
Comparing Types of Property

Property investment can form the basis for building wealth better than any other investment I know. But to go and purchase any property at all, and expect it to fulfil your expectations of becoming wealthy, is foolhardy – you wouldn't buy acreage in the Sahara Desert, would you? What type of property *is* good as an investment?

Although most property (within reason) has the features of a good investment – namely good capital growth, regular income, tax advantages, good security, liquidity, and personal control, some types of property fall down in one or two of these areas. Let's examine the main types of property – commercial, vacant land and residential – to see how they perform in these areas. Then you will begin to understand why it is that I have selected residential property as the key to building wealth.

Commercial Property

Commercial property covers a variety of properties and can be further divided into four groups – commercial, industrial, retail and hospitality. Commercial property, in the strict use of the word, includes office blocks in the Central Business District (CBD) as well as in suburban shopping centres. Offices belonging to doctors, solicitors and other professionals make up the bulk of commercial property.

Industrial property is comprised of a diverse group of buildings such as concrete batching plants, breweries and petro-chemical plants. It can also include the more familiar collection of tin sheds from which mechanics, panel beaters and the like operate. Retail property is a mixed group and varies from giants such as Coles and K-Mart, to the local corner store or newsagent. Hospitality covers a very broad range of properties, including hotels and motels as well as restaurants and entertainment centres.

Because they cost so much, commercial properties are usually owned by large financial institutions. In fact, 95% of the CBD in Australian capital cities is owned by these large financial institutions, such as trusts and insurance companies. However, some suburban commercial property is owned by small individual investors.

Commercial properties can produce strong capital growth and very high rent yields, primarily because the tenant pays all the outgoings (rates, etc). Another plus, is that the tenant usually takes pride in keeping the building looking attractive for his own business purposes, and this reduces the overall maintenance costs to you.

However, one of the biggest drawbacks of commercial property is the largely uncontrollable vacancy factor. Because large parcels of money are involved, and because it is so closely associated with the level of economic activity, commercial property is subject to the ravages of over and under supply on a grand scale. Consequently, commercial property can sometimes be vacant for several years. This may not be of grave concern to a large institutional investor with an unlimited source of cash, but for the small investor, it can be disastrous. In 1991, during the economic downturn, one in five shops in some suburbs of Sydney was vacant and at times, the vacancy factor for CBD offices was more than 25%.

This means that commercial property is suitable for only a small percentage of investors. A great deal more effort, experience and expertise is needed to monitor and assess all the risks, particularly those relating to the vacancy rate. If the vacancy rate can be controlled and minimised, then commercial property should provide you with the basis of a sound property portfolio. Some of the factors to be considered are:

Price structure

The value of commercial property is directly related to the rent levels and is reflected in the capitalisation rates. (Capitalisation rate or cap rate = rent / value of the property.) Maintaining high rent levels should ensure that the value of the property is maintained.

Tenant's business

Almost 80% of small businesses do not survive their early years of operation, so it is very important to have the right business tenant. The success of the tenant's business will ensure the success of your property investment. The rent can often be aligned to the turnover of the tenant's business, which further emphasises the need to find the right tenant.

Location

The location of commercial property is important so that it suits the needs of a particular tenant. If the tenant is in the fast food business, it would be in no one's best interests to be located three streets back from the main highway. A good understanding of the tenant's client base, and the exposure required, is a must if both of you are to survive.

Internal fittings

The plant equipment and fittings are usually supplied by the tenant. Often you will need to add extras – such as security grills on windows or air-conditioning.

Lease

The lease conditions must be predetermined and usually require the services of a competent solicitor. Whether the rent is tied to the CPI, or whether there is an option to carry on the lease at the end of the initial period are all factors that must be considered.

External risks

There are many risks that are beyond your control, which can seriously affect the livelihood of your tenant, and consequently your property. For example, during a recent visit to the Sunshine Coast in Queensland, I went looking for the local building society. When I finally located the office, there was a "For Lease" sign on the window of the shop in question and a notice saying "Moved to K-mart centre opposite". There were also "For Lease" signs on every shop nearby. Obviously, a new shopping centre had a drastic impact on all shops in the area, a factor beyond the control of the property owner.

Security

The risk associated with commercial property is recognised by the financial institutions who take a conservative approach to lending on the security of commercial property. Because commercial properties are valued on their rent (capitalisation rate), which may fluctuate, property values may also fluctuate. Therefore, many financial institutions will not lend on commercial property, while others will lend up to only 70% of the value.

Vacant Land

Vacant land may have no specific use, or it may be income-producing if used for example, for rural purposes. Prime vacant land can sometimes experience strong capital growth greater than 10% per year. Usually, large tracts of vacant land that adjoin suburban developments, have extremely good long-term growth potential. In the short-term, they may be a continual drain on cash resources, but over a 20 year period, the capital growth can be astronomical.

However, because vacant land does not produce any income, any expenses associated with it (including that of interest on the borrowings) would not be tax deductible against income from other sources. Consequently, vacant land does not have the attractive tax benefits of income-producing property. This minimises the effect of leverage and makes borrowing less effective than for income-producing property. Clearly, the loss of tax benefits has to be weighed up against the future potential capital growth. In the majority of cases, the foregone tax benefits substantially impair the capacity to acquire more property.

Rural property can provide some tax benefits if it is income-producing. However, because the yields are usually very low and the risks very high, it is generally only large companies who are able to hold onto such low-income-producing property in anticipation of future rezoning prospects.

Residential Property

Many investors ignore residential investment property simply because it is not glamorous. However, good investment returns are not necessarily associated with glamorous exteriors. In contrast to commercial property, *residential investment property is for all investors.* Most people have a basic understanding of housing needs and the value of residential real estate, whereas not everyone is able to gauge the business potential or the value of commercial property.

The vacancies associated with residential property are controllable to a much larger degree than commercial property and even when the vacancy factor is quite high, provision can be made to lessen the impact. This may involve reducing the rent level or improving the property to make it more desirable.

In poor economic conditions, businesses are usually the first to be affected and many will close down causing high vacancy rates in commercial property. However, despite a downturn in the business sector, people must still live somewhere. Consequently residential investment property is less severely affected in recessionary times. The fact that many financial institutions lend up to 90% of the value of residential property is testimony to the high regard they have for the security of such property.

But if residential property is such a great investment, why is it that commercial property and shares receive most of the attention in the newspapers? You may get the distinct impression that these are the best investments simply because they dominate the news scene. But not so, says an article that appeared in The Weekend Australian in May 26–27, 1990.

REPORT CASTS DOUBT ON RESIDENTIAL RATING

Residential property has long been thought of as one of the worst-performing forms of capital investment available.

It has been ranked behind commercial property, fixed interest, bonds and shares as an investment.

However a recent report by property analyst BIS Shrapnel Pty Ltd has cast doubt on this rating.

The report was commissioned by property developer Maksam Pty Ltd, which has been undertaking research to determine in which direction the company should expand.

It concludes that institutions and large private investors have tended to avoid investment in residential property because of the small size of the investments and the difficulty of managing the properties.

However the report says returns from residential investment are excellent in the longer term, a fact that has been ignored by larger investors. – – –

The BIS Shrapnel report says the long term growth available in residential property has out stripped shares, commercial property and fixed term investments.

Looking at capital growth alone, residential property performed better than either shares or commercial property in the last cycle. – – – –

The report says that immediate prospects for growth in residential property are good. – – – –

However, BIS Shrapnel fails to make any predictions for the sharemarket, saying: "It is clear that there will be major winners and losers in different sectors of the market during the next few years, corresponding to the differing prospects for the industries."

Residential property is a different story.

The evidence tendered by BIS Shrapnel in the report indicates that the last boom in Sydney was only stopped by the Federal Government acting to tighten money supply.

BIS Shrapnel forecasts that as soon as these constraints are removed, and interest rates fall, the Sydney residential property market will recover and show a growth of about 40% during the next three years.

If you need further convincing that residential property can be the best investment, just read the following report that appeared in the September 21, 1990 issue of the Business Review Weekly.

AMP Plunges into Residential Property.

The AMP society and its actuaries spent almost two years coming to terms with the fact that residential property can produce returns that are comparable with, or better than, other investments.

Much to its surprise, the numbers stack up.

The AMP announced last week that it was investing $145 million in a portfolio of 1,000 houses in Sydney's western and outer-western suburbs, to be managed by the NSW Department of Housing.

It marks the AMP's first venture into the residential sector.

The accompanying graph (not reproduced here) *shows that on a net return basis, the return from residential property, chartered over 20 years, outperforms equities, property trusts, bonds and index bonds.*

This finding has changed institutional investors view's of residential investment. – – – –

The NSW deal is a landmark – regarded as a breakthrough. – – – –

The financing technique frees the NSW Government from funding the capital costs of building 1,000 houses. – – – –

The agreement provides for the houses to be sold from the 14th to the 21st year. – – – –

The houses are being built now and will be priced at $100,000 – $140,000. – – – –

John Edwards says there is an element of "blue sky" in this deal. Considering Sydney's well-documented land shortage, together with projections that the city's population will rise by 1.6 million people by 2011, the residential sector must see a "substantial rise" in value, he says.

What more can be said to substantiate residential property as the basis for building wealth through investment property? I hope that these articles with their compelling arguments help to give you the confidence you need to use residential property as the prime vehicle for building wealth through investment property.

The most important points to emerge from these two articles are that:

- The returns from residential property can be greater than all other forms of investment.
- The prospects for the sharemarket are uncertain.
- The most suitable investment properties are in the lower end of the market.
- Long-term investment (14–21 years) is the way to go.
- Governments welcome private investment in residential property to help alleviate the public housing problem.
- Some superannuation funds are now investing in residential property.
- Commercial property developers are now recognising the value of developing residential property.
- Management problems associated with small investments can be overcome.
- Highly respected sources have now recognised the advantages of residential property as an investment.

7
Which Residential Property?

What sort of residential property should you buy for investment? Not only should you consider the attributes of the property, which are discussed in the following pages, but you must also consider your own financial personality. When it comes to choosing an investment property, no two people are alike. What's perfect for you may not be perfect for someone else. Your comfort level is important, and to this end, you should also consider how involved you want to be with the property.

Obviously, the more you are involved, the greater the financial return, but it isn't necessary to squeeze every last dollar from your investment property to achieve great returns. Learn to recognise your own level of involvement and delegate accordingly. You can paint, collect the rent, build the carport and fix the taps, or simply sit back and appoint a property manager who'll organise all these things to be done for you. Below are some of the questions you need to ask yourself to help you understand your own profile as an investor.

Do you want to be involved with a body corporate?
(Units and townhouses usually operate under a body corporate.)

How often do you want to be concerned with painting?
(Timber properties need to be painted every few years.)

Do you enjoy organising tradesmen?
(Newer properties require fewer repairs than older properties.)

Do you want to be able to drive past your property once a week?
(A property in your own suburb is more easily accessible.)

There is no single type of investment property that is substantially better than any other. The economic performance of a low-set brick in the outer suburbs may match that of an old terrace house in the inner city, but some investors swear by the former and others prefer the latter. Examples in the Appendix show you how totally different properties may produce similar rates of return. While some will cost you more along the way for better gains at the end, others cost very little along the way, for lower end gains.

Below is a list of the attributes of property to be considered. Not all of the more desirable attributes will be found in the one property and sometimes it may be a case of trading off the better attributes for the price. For example, although residential properties on main roads are not usually considered to be good rental propositions, a substantial reduction in the price may still make it a viable investment.

Location

Capital growth of 10% per year or more may be achievable in most areas where there is a stable and diverse economy. Therefore, cities and large provincial areas are preferable to very small country towns with a population of a few hundred people, and where the economy may be based on a single factor.

There is an element of luck in selecting the suburb that will return you the highest growth. However, rather than spending months travelling around from suburb to suburb trying to ascertain the "best" area, I firmly believe in purchasing in an area with which you are acquainted. If at all possible, choose your property within a 15 km radius of where you live, because of your familiarity with property prices and your ability to keep a close eye on your investment. Of course, this is not always feasible, particularly if you live in an upmarket area such as Sydney's North Shore. There will be many investors from both Melbourne and Sydney who must look farther afield to a different suburb of their city, or even interstate, to find appropriate rental property.

Once the general area is decided, the locality must be examined in terms of the attractions and detractions of the immediate environment. In general, tenants dislike properties that have the following detractions:

- on a busy road
- bus stop at front gate
- unsealed road at front door
- next door to schools
- adjacent to industrial sheds
- across the road from a large sporting complex
- railway at back fence
- large shopping complex next door
- next door to public toilets
- overpowering unit complexes on both sides

Properties should be "handy", but not necessarily "prime" (i.e. it is not necessary for a property to be one street back from the shopping centre, providing it is handy to transport, schools, shops, parks, and areas of employment).

It is often stated that property should be chosen for position, position, position. This is a gross over-statement, for while position is important, so many other factors must also be considered. Financial considerations are of utmost importance. I have seen investors purchase prime property solely on the basis of position. However, while the capital growth should be assured, the overall financial returns to the investor have been so poor that they negate any capital growth.

For instance, an investor I knew related the story of how he bought a prime residential property that was expected to become a future commercial development. He borrowed the entire amount of $250,000 at an interest rate of 19% with yearly payments of almost $50,000. Then he found that nobody wanted to rent the property because of the nearby noisy heavy machinery associated with the development. He kept the property for two years and eventually sold it for $350,000. In the mean time, the interest payments, which had been capitalised over that time, had increased the initial borrowings to more than $350,000. The point I'm making is that *all* aspects need to be considered, not just position, position, position.

Price

There are no hard and fast rules when it comes to price. I have a strong preference for properties in the bottom quarter of the market, wherever that might be. Currently in Brisbane this is $90,000– $150,000 or in Sydney, $120,000 – $200,000. If you live in a small provincial town, the bottom quarter of the market could be much less. There are many reasons for choosing a property in this price bracket.

Firstly, the lower price makes the property more affordable and the yield tends to be slightly higher. It does not follow that if a $100,000 property rents for $150 per week, a $400,000 property should rent for $600 per week (it will more likely be $400 per week). In general, the higher the price tag, the lower the yield.

Secondly, because of the lower rent, you have a greater selection of tenants who can afford to pay, so when economic times are down, there will always be tenants in search of the cheaper properties. Higher-priced properties may not only sit vacant for longer periods of time, but the rent may have to be lowered to attract any tenant at all.

Finally, should you wish to sell, properties in the bottom quarter of the market are more readily saleable. They attract first-home buyers as well as other investors. But this is not to say that you shouldn't buy a $500,000 property in an upmarket area – *if* the figures stack up.

For some properties, you can readily determine whether the price is reasonable or not by looking at the capitalisation rates (cap. rate). For flats and multi-tenanted units, the value of the property may be reasonably ascertained by capitalising the rent at whatever is the current market cap. rate. For example, a block of flats returning $22,000, showing an 11% yield, would have a capitalised value of $200,000 ($22,000 x 100)/11. For outer suburban houses, the yield is usually 4 to 9%. Although this may appear fairly low, the real return is much higher and is calculated on the cash flow of the property (see Appendix).

Many investors are under the mis-apprehension that higher priced properties have a higher capital growth. While it is true that the amount of capital gain may be higher, the percentage may still be the same. For example, if a $250,000 property experiences growth of 10%, the gain is $25,000. Compare this to an $80,000 property where a 10% capital gain is smaller at $8,000. However, in both cases, the percentage growth is still the same.

Physical Attributes

Some of the more important factors you need to consider are:

Construction style

The style of the property (i.e flats, units, townhouses or single houses) largely determines the type of tenant you are seeking. For example, an expensive upmarket townhouse may suit a professional couple with lavish tastes, and a suburban low-set brick house is very suitable for families with mum, dad, two kids and a dog.

Construction material

Whether the exterior is constructed of brick, weatherboard, fibro, or chamferboard etc, you must consider both the maintenance factor and the price. For example, a weatherboard house bought for $95,000 may prove to be just as good an investment as a $110,000 low-set brick. I have no preference for one or the other because paints today are fairly sophisticated and non-brick houses should only need painting about once in 10 years.

Condition

The condition of the property must be related to the price and to your desire to be involved with repairs. While the property must be structurally sound (a building inspection will be worth your while), cosmetic repairs may be all that is needed. If you are the handyman type, you may achieve a great deal of enjoyment by maintaining the property yourself. If not, a more expensive property in much better condition, and requiring much less maintenance, may be preferable.

Age

The age of the building can affect maintenance, but just as important are the tax implications relating to the capital allowance claims. These are discussed in chapter 15, but basically, new properties receive a 2.5% allowance. However, this is not the sole criterion for selecting a new property or not, but one of the many considerations.

Land size

Land size will depend on your choice of unit, flat or house as well as location. Properties of at least 20 perches are desirable in suburbia, but with the trend towards cluster housing, smaller sizes are becoming more acceptable. Some inner city properties may be as little as 8 perches (200 square metres). Because the scarcity factor acts on the land content, it's possible that property with a higher land content has a slightly higher capital growth. This, however must be weighed up against the overall price, maintenance and rent levels.

Land features

Look for easy-to-maintain yards, because most tenants do not wish to spend their leisure hours maintaining intricate gardens. Swimming pools can be a hassle for both you and the tenant. While corner sites provide better access to multi-tenanted dwellings, our experience with normal suburban blocks has shown them to be noisier and a lot more difficult to maintain because of the additional footpaths.

Building size

The size of the building must be considered in relation to prospective tenants, price and location. Inner city properties vary from one-bedroom flats to many-bedroomed houses. While in the suburbs, three-bedroom houses tend to dominate. Also, just because you like to have an ensuite and family room in your own home, it doesn't mean that your rental property needs them as well.

Car accommodation

It may suffice to have off-street parking with inner city properties, but it is usually better for suburban properties to have a garage or at least a carport. Quite often, tenants are in the process of building their own house, and a closed-in lockable garage is a very desirable attribute as a storage area.

Fencing

Fencing is a distinct advantage in suburbia but again, it depends on your tenant market. It makes your property appeal to a wider selection of tenants who may have children or pets to consider.

Building aspect

The aspect of the building does not necessarily affect the property valuations, but it is very important to have a property that is comfortable for your tenants. In hot climates, tenants dislike hot houses so lounge, kitchen, and dining room combinations should be away from the afternoon sun. The tenancy can often be prolonged if the tenants are comfortable.

Internal fittings

There is no need to have lavish fittings in a tenanted property, but it is important to make the property as attractive as possible. Such fittings as curtains are fairly standard and add to the comfort of tenants. Most tenants expect nice floors or floor coverings, and kitchen cupboards need only be clean and functional. Built-in wardrobes are usually standard in new buildings, but for older ones without built-ins, it is inexpensive to supply one or two wardrobes.

Furniture

I prefer unfurnished investment properties because tenants tend to treat your building with the same respect as their own furniture. Good tenants should have accumulated some assets in the way of furniture, and those without any furniture at all would make you wonder why. Also, if tenants have their own furniture, they tend to move less often because of the effort and expense.

Zoning

Different councils have different zoning regulations that could limit or enhance your options later, but don't speculate on possible rezonings. Too many investors buy houses with a "higher use" zoning (suitable for units or commerce etc), but rarely do they achieve better returns and usually the property is on-sold "as is".

Emotions

Do not let your emotions dominate your choice of rental property. Too many investors buy with their heart rather than a calculator. Property investment and building wealth is about dollars and cents, not colours of curtains. If you have assessed the property as an excellent investment, except for the purple curtains and the terrible dog next door, go with the figures. If you are buying property for the long-term, most of these things won't be around after a few years.

A Typical Residential Investment Property

Despite the notion that we would all like a recipe for the ideal rental property – there *is* no such property. The guidelines outlined in this chapter should give you an idea of what to look for but as pointed out earlier, there are countless factors to be considered. To give you an idea of the disparity in properties that ultimately serve the same wealth building purpose, I have described two of our own investment properties. Both the properties are close to Brisbane and neither was bought with a specific description in mind.

House A

Currently valued at around $120,000, this property is an older style worker's cottage on 40 perches (1,000 square metres) of very desirable land in a quiet location near the seaside. The house itself is weatherboard and on timber stumps. The kitchen is older style with removable cupboards, and none of the three bedrooms have built-ins. Four wardrobes have been placed in the bedrooms. The bathroom is small and in the same condition as when it was first built fifty years ago. A double carport was recently added. Rent is now $150 per week and long-term I expect that the property will have capital growth greater than the norm, primarily because of the land content and its good position. However, this anticipated higher capital growth will most likely be offset by higher maintenance costs.

House B

This suburban low-set brick house is on 24 perches (around 600 sq. metres) in a quiet street and is currently valued at around $100,000. The value of the house is about half that of the house and land. Everything about the house is modern, being only three years old, but it is small – a very basic 10 square home with a small single carport. Two of the three bedrooms have built-in wardrobes. Rent is now $155 per week and I anticipate average growth of around 10%, but the property will need minimal maintenance.

Which type is best? *Both!* The difference between the two properties lies in the fact that House B provides more net income with standard capital growth, while the older House A provides less net income in return for potentially greater capital gains. In the long term, both will have produced pretty much the same overall returns in excess of 30%. (The Appendix will show you how to analyse the rates of return from different properties and explain how you can use a computer program to make this process quick and easy.)

8
Buying for Keeps

Building wealth through residential investment property is so simple that it is often overlooked. Someone once asked me what I do in the property industry, and I replied that I show investors how to invest in property. "Is that all?" he said, and continued with, "That's easy. All you do is buy a property and flog it off when the price goes up." – Wrong!

It's a shame that this is the thinking pattern of many "investors" in property. It's also the reason why none of them ever become wealthy because true wealth takes time. Over time, you harness the power of debt and compound capital growth to build real wealth. I will emphasise again our philosophy. Building wealth through investment property is achieved, not through buying and selling, but through buying and keeping properly financed residential property. This is what distinguishes *investing* in property from *trading* in property.

Property Traders

Trading involves buying real estate and selling at a profit within a short time. Hopefully, when all the costs are accounted for, there is a healthy return that makes it all worth while. But a property trader and a property investor are about as similar as a milkman and a dairy farmer. The only thing the milkman and the dairy farmer have in common is milk. And likewise, the only thing that property traders and investors have in common is real estate. But there the similarity ends.

Trading in property is NOT investing in property. Unfortunately, many of the books on the subject of property investment are really about property trading. They describe in great detail how to negotiate a bargain, how to renovate, and how to pick the best time to buy and sell. Now I'm not saying that you can't make money by trading in property – but it is a specialist's occupation and requires expert skills in many different areas. Successful traders spend all day, every day, living, breathing and talking about property as a merchandisable commodity. Property trading is a job – not a pastime – but a full-time career.

Some people expect to make money by trading in real estate simply because they think they know everything about it. They live in a house or unit, walk on land and touch it everyday and thereby assume that being familiar is synonymous with being an expert. However, being familiar with property does not imply expertise in trading. You probably know how to have a bet on the horses. But do you know enough about horses to buy and sell them at a profit? You'd probably never dream of trying to make money by trading in horses.

And likewise with property. Knowing a little bit about property does not automatically imply expertise in property trading. For most people, their skills are usually limited to one subject area. And no matter if you're a teacher, mechanic, doctor or farm labourer, when the day is done, you can't expect to wave a magic wand and become an expert kitchen renovator or rezoning expert. Neither can you be expected to pick the best time to buy and sell property. It's far better to use your skills in your normal job to generate the money to plough into long-term property investment.

A friend of mine is a talented and dedicated teacher and he was totally convinced (before meeting me) that he could make a lot of money buying and selling property. He spent many a night painting and renovating the few properties he owned in readiness to sell them. Each year, he not only paid tax on his income as a teacher, but tax on any gains he may have made from the sale of the properties. He exhausted himself both mentally and physically trying to make money from property trading, until finally he realised he would have been far better off to have kept all the properties he had bought. Not only would he have saved paying all that extra tax, but he could have been getting a healthy tax refund.

Traders include renovators, speculators and developers who trade full time in property and it is important to distinguish clearly between their role and that of the true investor.

Renovators

Full time property renovators can take a run-down property and transform it into something beautiful and more valuable. They spend all day every day working in a mess, but they know exactly how much money they can afford to spend on improvements so that it remains a viable proposition. They know all the tricks of the trade, and have a great ability to improve property cosmetically with the least expense. Usually, renovators possess a trade such as carpentry or plumbing so that the labour costs are minimised. Sometimes they live in the property and endure the sawdust and the paint fumes while they carry out the renovations.

Speculators

Then there are the professional property speculators. They may spend all day in their car with a car-phone by their side just waiting to pounce on that bargain. They are known to all the local real estate agents and are totally familiar with prices and market conditions. Speculators live by their wits – and should be clearly distinguished from long-term investors.

Developers

Developers are full time property traders who totally alter the original characteristics of property and then on-sell. For example, land developers buy land, rezone and subdivide, add water, power, phone, road and sewage connections, and eventually sell. Or for unit developers, land may be rezoned to accommodate a higher density of housing.

Traders versus Investors

There are factors that are crucial to the success of a trading project, but which are almost unimportant to long-term property investors. Buying property long-term is a matter of buying reasonably priced property with appropriate finance at any reasonable time. Not so with trading. There are many fine points to be considered and more than likely "reasonable" is not the operative word. Everything must be judged accurately down to the last detail and "spot on" would more aptly describe the conditions under which traders operate. Some of the more important "spot on" factors are as follows.

Timing

Timing is critical to property traders and any little hiccup in the market can play havoc with a trader's profits. However, investing in property long-term means that timing is of little consequence. Even though the property market may move in cycles, investing long-term has the effect of ironing out the humps and bumps. So you don't have to be a *when to* investor when you buy property to keep long-term. And you should not be concerned with what the property is worth by next year or the year after, but rather – what it will be worth when you retire?

Loans

Property loans for traders have to be flexible so that they can sell at short notice, and there is usually little chance of fixing the interest rate for a lengthy period. This leaves traders extremely vulnerable to interest rate fluctuations, which can destroy a potentially good proposition. Long-term property investors can look for cheaper, but less flexible loans where they can fix the interest rate and remain insulated from wild fluctuations.

Price

One of the real factors that traders need to consider at the outset is the price. Everyone loves a bargain and when you buy and sell property, the initial price can make or break a deal. However, when you buy long-term, you only need to pay fair market value to achieve good growth.

Costs

As well as the costs that may be incurred in renovating or developing a property, there are also the selling costs that include agent's commissions, solicitor's fees and possibly mortgage adjustment costs (discussed in more detail in chapter 14). The interest on the money borrowed is a real cost that must be accounted for. For long-term investors, these costs would be insignificant compared to long-term gains.

Taxation

The tax implications for traders versus investors are totally different. Trader's profits are taxed at marginal tax rates, so taxes can wipe out any cream. There is no fixed time factor before you are classified as a trader. And if you have been buying and selling property consistently, you may have to pay the full tax on property after even five or six years with no allowance for inflation! Not only are long-term investors saving tax by borrowing money and using the negative gearing laws to gain a tax refund, the capital gains tax (see chapter 14) favours long-term investors by taxing only gains above inflation.

Long-Term Investment

I hope that by now you can see that trading in property is not investing in property. This book is not about how to find a bargain; nor is it about how to renovate a property or how to rezone land and then build a block of units. There are many books on the market written on these topics. This is not one of them. Instead, it is all about how average people can build wealth through investing long-term in residential property. But it takes time – time to take advantage of the compound capital growth of property and to reap the rewards in the future.

Investing in property can be boring – like watching the tide come in. Initially though, it can be so exciting finding the property, arranging the finance, doing minor renovations if needed, and then finally organising the tenants. And then there's nothing to do – which is when most people are vulnerable to an attack of "Fidget Fever". People can't sit back and wait. They have to dabble with their property, add an extension that's not really necessary, renovate when it's not necessary, and then quite often sell it

when it's not necessary, just to see what it's worth. Believe me, it's very
hard to keep away from that property and allow it to build your wealth,
slowly but surely. Of course you have to manage both the property and
your finances, but for the rest of the time, leave it be. It's far better to get
on with your own job, the one you know best, and make extra money to
pour back into investment property for your future. St Vincent de Paul
summed it all when he said:

"All comes at the proper time to him who knows how to wait."

Buying property to keep is a whole new way of thinking for most
people. Yet when people talk about superannuation, they immediately
think in phrases like retirement package, future security, income assurance,
nest egg, and a time frame usually between 10 and 30 years. It's time to
use these cliches when you're talking about property, because property can
be the best form of "superannuation", the best "pension fund" and the best
"insurance fund" that you'll ever have.

Let me ask you – when you buy a "normal" superannuation plan, I
mean one offered by an institution, do you ring up every few months to
find out what it's worth? Do you change from one plan to another just for
the sake of it? Do you fiddle with it and tinker with it night and day to see
how you can make it better? Do you plan to keep it for just a little while
and then cash it in? Of course not. So if property is to provide you with
all those things you want from superannuation – then it must be kept
long-term.

It's noteworthy that when AMP purchased $145 million of residential
property in Sydney in 1990, they planned to keep it for periods of between
14 and 21 years. If this is the life span that the large institutions see fit to
keep property, then it should be the time frame you are looking at for your
own superannuation scheme using property.

"If I buy property to keep long-term, when do I get to see my money?"
is the question people ask when they become aware of this buy and keep
principle. I usually answer with another question. "What do you want to
see your money for?" Isn't the whole reason for investing to have future
wealth and security? Then, when your property has grown in value by so
much, and the rent has outstripped your interest payments, you should be
receiving a nice income from your tenants. And it goes up with inflation.
So why sell?

When your investment property increases in value, rather than selling
"just to see how much it's worth", you should be borrowing against the
increased equity to buy more property – and more.

PART III

The Framework for Building Wealth

9
Getting Started –
Your Own Home

There is one point on which most investment advisors agree – your first investment should be your own home. In any financial plan you must start somewhere, and the most obvious place to start is at your own doorstep. Owning your home is the great Australian dream and probably is part of our primordial instincts to stake out our own territory.

It also offers financial independence that is second to none and provides you ultimately with a place to live, where the only commitments are the relatively small expenses of rates, insurance and maintenance. It currently provides one of the few tax havens left untouched by the Government, because it is not subject to the capital gains tax. Most people agree that the emotional benefits of home ownership are just as important as the economic considerations. Home ownership creates a sense of worth, and a sense of security that no rented home can give. It provides stability for the family unit and for children growing up. Maintaining the property is a satisfying experience and in the end, there is something to show for hard work and mortgage repayments.

Sadly, less than 70% of Australians own their home and despite well meaning governments, this percentage is declining. Owning your own home is just as difficult today, as it was yesterday, as it will be tomorrow. So the earlier you start, the better. Believe me, if you aspire to wealth through investing in property, the hardest of all the properties you buy will be your first. One of the biggest drawbacks of borrowing to buy your own home is that the interest on the loan is NOT tax deductible. And because you're paying mortgage repayments, living expenses *and* tax on your income, there seems very little left.

You need to lay the foundations and start saving for the deposit on that first property as soon as possible. Then when you've borrowed the remaining amount, get rid of that loan as quickly as possible. So the equity build up will provide you with an ever increasing net worth to the point where you eventually own your own home outright. There are many ways you can achieve home ownership and as I'll point out, your first property need not be your principal place of residence.

But it is just as important not to stop at just one property. Too many people stop when they have paid off one and never continue to build their wealth. One property is not enough for financial independence but it's certainly better to have one than none. Relatively speaking, you have taken just *one* step – albeit the biggest step – toward wealth. Even though you have free rent, there'll be no other income and the capital gain on the home you live in, can't feed you. Even if you sell, all other properties will have increased by approximately the same proportion. It's not until you own additional properties that your net wealth increases dramatically.

The increased equity in your own home should be used as a springboard to more wealth, not a stepping stone to more spending. After the last round of property price rises, one of the local bank managers told me how they had written record "equity" loans. However, those loans had been for boats and cars and other luxury items. The increased equity was spent on wealth-destroying consumer goods, rather than wealth-creating assets.

When you retire, even if you do own your home outright, where is the income going to come from to support your current lifestyle? You could move into a tent and rent out your home. That would certainly provide you with income, but wouldn't it be far better to build your wealth by acquiring more property? Below is a list of ideas that should help you get started on your road to wealth by getting you into your first property.

The Deposit

Saving for that first home should be a top priority, even while you are still at school. Unfortunately, buying nice cars and nice clothes and going to the movies seems so much more important to the young. If you spend everything when you are young, you suffer twice: once because you take longer to save the deposit for your first property, and twice because ingrained spending habits are hard to break. Worse still, by the time you realise your mistakes, the property costs more! Is it any wonder that many young couples never manage to accumulate a deposit for their own home, simply because they start too late? The traditional way of saving for a deposit and borrowing the remainder enables people to get a foothold into the property market. Starting with too small a deposit on too costly a property is the reason for most of the economic woes of many young families who are struggling to repay large mortgages. Small deposits on cheaper properties are OK, because the loan size is usually still manageable, but very small deposits on expensive homes can be a recipe for disaster. Big mortgage repayments leave the family vulnerable to changes in interest rates.

It is fairly simple for a young couple to save a large amount for a deposit if they start early. When two people are saving together, their combined savings over several years makes it that much easier to get a large deposit. But sadly, many Australians know nothing about saving money.

Let's stretch your imagination to find out just how much you, or your children, will need for a deposit in the future. We'll assume a property can be bought today for $100,000 and the deposit is 30%. You can see from the table below, how much deposit was needed in the past, and how much will be needed in the future if capital growth continues at around 10% per year. If you haven't already started saving for a deposit, start today.

How Much Deposit Do You Need?

Year	Property Value ($) (10% Growth per Year)	Deposit Needed ($) (30% of Property Value)
1952	$2,200	$660
1962	$6,000	$1,800
1972	$15,000	$4,500
1982	$40,000	$12,000
1992	**$100,000**	**$30,000**
2002	$260,000	$78,000
2012	$675,000	$202,500
2022	$1,750,000	$525,000

Realistic Expectations

One of the best ways to get into your first home is to buy an affordable property in the bottom end of the market. This enables the loan size to be kept to a minimum and allows your equity in the property to build up much faster. Even though your expectations are high and your aim is to own a mansion on the harbour eventually, you must start with the basics.

I recently met a young couple who lived in a $500,000 house in an upmarket suburb of Melbourne. They owned the house outright, even though they were both on very average incomes. The woman told me that they must have either been lucky, or had a good eye for real estate to have bought this property. But knowing her background I pointed out that they owed their comfort not to "Lady Luck", but to the fact that they were prepared to buy their first house at the bottom end of the market in a less than desirable suburb and move on from there.

Apart from too little deposit, one of the reasons that young couples get into trouble with variable interest rates and mortgage repayments is that for their first home, many will not settle for less than a brick house in an upmarket suburb, complete with double lock-up garage and ensuite.

Our first property was a very small seven square, high-set chamfer-board near the mudflats in Kippa Ring, a suburb on the outskirts of Brisbane. The bedrooms were so small that they looked like a walk-in-wardrobe of today. However, 20 years later, we still own that house and it is a first class rental property less than 500 metres from a huge shopping complex built some six years after we purchased the property. So aim high, but take one step at a time.

Mortgage Reduction

Once you have purchased a property with a substantial deposit, you should aim to pay out that loan as quickly as possible. Basically, this means paying as much as you can, as often as you can. Increased loan re-payments do not prevent you from recovering the money if needed. In an emergency, you simply arrange with the bank to stop further payments, until the excess payments have been used up.

Unfortunately, as I pointed out earlier, the interest payments on a home loan are not tax deductible, so all the money that goes into paying your mortgage must come from after-tax dollars. This is the prime reason why buying your first property is the hardest of all. As well as no tax relief, unlike rental property, there is no tenant to assist with interest payments. There are many ways of reducing your home mortgage and the following tips should help you achieve first-home ownership more quickly.

- Make a simple commitment to put money into your mortgage first and buy luxuries second. You can have all those luxuries later.
- Think carefully before upgrading to a new car, and avoid buying a second (re-read chapter 2). It is far cheaper to take a taxi somewhere several times a week than to own a second car. Cars are the biggest guzzlers of money, and figures from the RAC suggest that it can cost more than $100 per week just to run an older style car. Cars always seem to need something doing to them, usually when you have the least amount of spare money.

- Never buy consumer goods on credit. If you can't afford to pay cash for them, don't borrow the money. Reduce your use of credit cards. By all means have them, but restrict their use and always pay them back before the interest-free period is up. Buying consumer goods on credit is one sure way to financial ruin and does nothing to reduce your mortgage.

- Restrict the money you spend on your children, or even defer having children until you have established your wealth foundations. Children seem to have only two words in their vocabulary "I want". For many parents, this plea is difficult to ignore, particularly if you have had a deprived childhood yourself. But you will be doing your children a big favour by showing them restraint and teaching them the real value of money. Instead of succumbing to all the "I wants", point out what "I need". It's truly amazing how little it costs to entertain children when what they really want is attention.

On a recent trip to the Brisbane Exhibition, we took six children – our own as well as our friend's children. Each child was limited to $15 with which they had to buy lunch, show bags, rides and anything else they wanted. Very eagerly they watched the price of everything. Then quite accidentally, they stumbled across a stand where a bag of rubbish could be exchanged for a small reward such as chewing gum, a packet of twisties, or a small toy. The idea was to encourage children to clean up the grounds. For more than two hours, our six children picked up rubbish and collected their small reward after filling each bag. We had to drag them away in the end but by then, each child had gathered up enough rubbish to "earn" a dozen prizes. What a simple pleasure – and so cheap! My children still maintain that "picking up rubbish" was the highlight of the show.

- Holidays need not be extravagant and a small cottage near the sea is a fraction the cost of a high rise unit on the Gold Coast, but provides just as much fun and relaxation.

- Mortgage-offset accounts effectively save you paying tax on the interest on your savings, while reducing the principal on your home loan. But rather than use these, I believe it is better to pay out the mortgage with most of your available cash, and then reduce the payments when and if needed.

There are many techniques to help you pay out your mortgage but all require the right mental attitude. Try to get away from the "I want it now" mentality and replace it with, "I will have it all later" thinking. When you become wealthy through investing in real estate, you will be able to have all the things you want now – and much more.

Adding Value

One way of improving your financial situation is to add value to your existing property by either extending or renovating the building, or simply by landscaping the grounds. Usually, people want a finished house that looks great right from the start. The problem is that the value is already added in to the price with little room for improvements and adding value. The best way to add value is to buy the basic shell of a property (either a small new one or a run-down old one), and add improvements to it in your own time with your own money (not borrowed). It's even better if you can do the work yourself. However, be careful not to over-capitalise on a property if you are adding value. There is no sense in paying $20,000 for a new kitchen, if the property is worth only $80,000 to start with.

Moving Upmarket

If you continue to add value to your property, there is only a certain amount of value you can add before you over-capitalise. The next step should be to begin to increase your net worth further by buying rental property. However there are those who wish to choose the "upgrade path". This is achieved by selling the property you have just improved and then buying into an even better property with the potential to add more value. If this is done several times, eventually you could finish up with a large mansion. The advantage in doing this is that any capital gain should be tax free, because current tax laws exempt the principal place of residence from capital gains tax.

The only time you should ever contemplate selling property is when you are building equity in this manner. There are plenty of books on the subject of how to buy, how to renovate and how to present your property when you sell. Suffice to say that it is just one method of building equity and that it will only suit some young couples.

However, although the upgrade path is a good way of building equity, I don't believe it is the most efficient way of building wealth. If you are working and paying large amounts of tax, this method does not provide personal tax relief at all and furthermore, your improvements are paid for from after-tax dollars. There's not much point in living in a mansion if you have no other assets to support you when you retire. Sooner or later, you'll need to down-grade to a cheaper property so that some of the capital can be released to provide that retirement income for you. I believe it is far better to remain in a comfortable property and build wealth through investment property by using the rent and tax benefits to help you.

First Property not Your Home

Your first property need not be your own home. If you are still living with Mum and Dad (with cheap rent and board), you could take advantage of this and make your first home an investment property.

Even if you are renting a property with several others, it is often more economical to stay put, pay your share of the rent, and then buy a rental property. Care needs to be taken if, at some stage, you want to move into the property, because the tax laws allow negative gearing providing there is a foreseeable income from the property. If you keep the property as an investment, there should be no problem.

A variation on this theme is to take in boarders who will help pay the interest bill. Many young people already do this, but go to great lengths to conceal the rent from the Taxation Office. What they don't realise is that they would be far better off if they declared the income and claimed a portion of the interest as a tax deduction, thereby obtaining a tax refund.

For example, if you took in three boarders, you would be able to claim three-quarters of the interest, as well as three-quarters of the depreciation on fittings within the house, and three-quarters of the electricity, phone, rates and maintenance (see chapter 15). Likewise, if there were six boarders, you would be able to claim six-sevenths of the expenses. The limit is set only by council regulations and how long you wish to queue for a shower. The only drawback is that the property is no longer free of capital gains tax. This should not be too much of a concern because the tax saved in the interim period may far outweigh the potential capital gains tax of the future – which will be nothing if you don't sell.

If your parents have already embarked on their wealth building plan and have bought an investment property, it could be an ideal opportunity to make use of the situation by renting it from them. Providing the rent is at a reasonable level, you would have the perfect opportunity to get ahead and they would have the satisfaction of getting a good tenant – you. You then could buy your own rental property, and take advantage of all its inherent tax benefits.

One way for parents to help you buy investment property without giving you cash, is for them to allow you to use their property as security for a loan. In this way you can borrow the full amount for an investment property without having a cash deposit.

10
Building Wealth

Now that you have read this far, you should be well on your way to understanding that the principle of building wealth through investment property involves borrowing, buying and then keeping income-producing residential property for your future financial independence. But it's now time to look in more detail at how it all works. When a builder builds a house, he needs a plan. When a rally driver takes to the road, he needs a map. And when you build wealth through investment property, you'll need a strategy.

The strategy can be varied according to your age, circumstances, your desire to spend a little extra on luxuries along the way, and how soon you want to get there. How much money you divert into building your wealth depends on balancing your immediate needs with your future desires.

It's a bit like dieting. If you follow the diet strictly to the letter, you'll lose a certain amount of weight in a certain amount of time. If, however, you are human and deviate from the diet by indulging in pizza once a week or a glass of wine every night, you can still achieve a weight loss, but it just takes a little longer.

So too with investing. If you want to continue having a holiday in the snow each year, that's fine. If you want to buy a nice car – that's fine too. It simply prolongs the time it takes to build wealth. Somewhere between rigidly sticking to a wealth-building plan and spending all your money on luxuries, you'll find a happy medium that suits your particular lifestyle. Henry David Thoreau made an accurate judgement of human nature when he said:

"That man is richest whose pleasures are the cheapest."

Firstly, I'll give you a large-scale map of the strategy for success so that you can broadly see where you're going. This strategy will show you in three steps, how to achieve financial independence through investment property. Then I'll get down to a finer scale map by showing you, using a typical young couple as an example, how to figure your way to a million dollars net worth in just 10 years – all on an average income.

Strategy for Success

The strategy used by us and many other successful property investors can be summarised in three steps. The first step is always the hardest – preparing to build a property portfolio by working towards your very first home. The second step of buying and accumulating properties takes at least 10 years and covers your working life. The third step is organising and managing your retirement and enjoying the fruits of your labour.

Step 1   Preparation for a property portfolio

- **Adopt sound financial principles:** From the beginning, you must adopt such basic financial principles as buying luxuries only after investment commitments are met. Don't try to keep up with the Joneses. Later, you'll have more than the Joneses ever dreamed of.

- **Get an income:** You need an income to support your borrowings, but it needn't be a high income. Even people in lowly paid jobs can achieve wealth through property investment. The income can be from your work or from any other investments.

- **Set a goal:** When are you going to start? When would you like to retire? How many properties will you need to give you the income you require? What luxuries do "need"? What sacrifices are you going to make on the way?

- **Start saving money:** The earlier you start saving for your own home, the better. Start while you're still at school, and when you're ready to buy your first home, you'll have a large deposit.

- **Buy your first home:** Using a large deposit, borrow to buy your first home and make sure it is a realistically priced property, without all the mod cons. They'll come later.

- **Establish equity in your own home:** Very simply, place as much money into your home loan as often as possible. This is a very difficult stage because you must pay *all* the interest bill on your home loan. The equity you build up can then be the stepping stone to more property. Although it's best to have a substantial equity in your own home (or even better, to own it outright) before you start buying more property, it's not essential. If you can handle payments on both your own loan and the investment property loan, then don't wait.

- **Be confident:** Many people know a few basic financial principles, most have some equity in their own home, and the majority of people work – but so few have the confidence to change their way of thinking and to make the next step.

Step 2   Building the property portfolio

- **Prepare a budget:** Do your sums so that you know how much investment property you can afford. Later in this chapter, I'll show you exactly how to prepare a budget.

- **Borrow against your equity:** You use the built up equity in your own home as a "deposit" to borrow the entire amount for your first investment property – no cash deposit is necessary and you can borrow all of the associated costs as well. Preferably, the loan should be interest-only with a fixed rate of interest.

- **Buy your first investment property:** The best investment property for you is income-producing residential property. Buy in the bottom quarter of the market in an area with which you are familiar, preferably in a larger city or town. The property should be handy, not prime, and nice enough to attract good tenants.

- **Let the property:** Preferably leave this to an experienced property manager, unless you are particularly adept at dealing with people.

- **Service the loan:** Paying the interest bill is made easier because the tenant and the taxman make your share of the interest bill small. It could well cost you less than $100 per week to buy this first rental property. Get a variation on your tax instalments (see chapter 16) to ease your cash flow.

- **Take precautions:** Cover yourself for all eventualities by taking every step possible to ensure your success (see chapter 17).

- **Be patient:** This is probably the most difficult. You have to wait for your property, your rent and your salary to increase before you take the next step. Your strategy is long-term, not short-term, so don't fall into the trap of selling "just to see how much you've made".

- **Gain knowledge:** Spend as much time as you can reading, asking questions and talking to other property investors.

- **Borrow more money:** Borrow more money by refinancing, using the increased equity in both your own home and the first investment property. And again, borrow interest-only and fix the interest rate.

- **Buy more properties:** Using the borrowed money from your refinancing, buy more and more properties – still using none of your own money. How quickly you accumulate property depends not only on the property growth, but mostly on the rate of increase in cash flow from both rents and your own salary. Over a period of 10 years you may accumulate up to seven, or even more rental properties.

Step 3 *Managing your property portfolio*

- **Decision time:** Once you have your collection of properties in place, you have the ability to sell, hold, or continue to buy more property, depending on your age and your expectations at this stage. Have you achieved enough? Do you want to continue working for just a bit longer? Do you want to work part time? Do you want to increase your spending so that you can enjoy a few more luxuries? Or do you just want to retire? The greatest thing about building wealth through investment property is that this decision may come much earlier in your life than through any other means.

- **Reduce debt:** Whatever your decision, you can manipulate the debt levels to whatever level you require, by selling a property or two to reduce the loan. This reduces the interest payments and will give you a positive cash flow from your properties. Perhaps you can use work-related superannuation monies to reduce or service the debt. As you are in control, the choice is yours.

- **Live on rental income:** At this stage, your property portfolio will become your primary source of income giving you total financial independence. Consider the situation if your goal was to achieve four properties, each worth $100,000, free of debt and rented at $160/week. (Note that these figures are in today's dollars, but projected into the future, would have the same purchasing power as the amounts listed here). This could provide direct income of about $26,000 per year clear of expenses ($32,000 gross less $6,000 expenses). And, what is more, the rents should rise with inflation.

- **Time to buy luxuries:** Selling a property may provide sufficient funds for a new car and an overseas holiday. Maybe you want to help your children. Or may be you just want to help others. By creating your own superannuation fund in the form of property, you can "cash in" whenever you wish. Wouldn't it be nice to have such financial security that the only problem you face is what to do with the money?

- **Avoid temptation:** Having built your wealth through investment property, there is a great temptation to "dabble" in other interesting things. Don't! I have seen many people set themselves up for life with residential investment property and then lose out completely by going into something with which they are totally unfamiliar – bug farming, entertainment centres – in fact, anything that just takes their fancy. Stay with what you have been successful at – residential rental property. By all means buy all those luxuries – but don't put your properties at risk.

Figuring Your Way

When I published my first manual on residential investment property, everyone understood the principles and the broad strategy for success, but many asked us the same questions on the finer detail:

How do I know when I can buy my next property?

And how do I know how many properties I can buy?

How do I know what level of debt will be comfortable?

What sort of income do I need?

How much money can I expect to make?

Can you give me some examples to show me how it works?

So what I'll do now is present a more detailed road map for everyone, so that you can see just what signposts to look for along your road to wealth. In so doing, we'll follow the progress over a 10 year period, of a typical young couple who have paid out the loan on their home. The figures I'll use will show you step by step, how, when rents and wages rise with time, they will have the ability to borrow more and more money, to purchase more and more property to build more and more net worth. Initially, they can afford to purchase two investment properties and then buy another one every two years. Eventually, they will have built up a net worth of more than a million dollars in just 10 years.

In your own situation, your income, rent, property values, interest rates and living expenses may vary. Also, the rate at which these values rise will differ according to market conditions and the area in which you live. So your road to wealth may be a little different, or a little slower or a little faster.

I liken it to a car trip between Sydney and Melbourne. The road map indicates that if you follow a particular route, the distance will be exactly 900 kilometres and if you travel at exactly 90 kilometres an hour, you will take exactly 10 hours to get there. Now we all know that this is highly improbable – you are definitely not going to travel at exactly the same speed all the way. There'll be stop signs, slow cars on the road, food stops and a whole host of other reasons why you will not arrive in exactly 10 hours. You may even want to detour to a friend's house on the way. Or you could take risks and travel at 100 kilometres per hour and get there much sooner. But no matter which way you go, or how long you take, you will eventually get there. And so it is with building wealth through investment property. Like the car journey – set a destination, draw a map and enjoy the trip, but be prepared to take your own time. Now let's get back to the young couple in our example.

The first step that our hypothetical couple must take is to prepare a budget for their first year. They have a total income of $45,000 (say the husband earns $40,000 and the wife $5,000) and they own their own home valued at $100,000. They currently pay tax of $11,250, and have living expenses of $15,500. They want to borrow to buy two rental properties, each worth $100,000 and to do this they can borrow the entire amount for the properties plus an extra $4,500 per property to cover costs. The total loan on each property is then $104,500, on which the interest is 14% or $14,630 per year (interest-only). Each property would rent for $160 per week ($8,320 per year). Let's look at their budget.

Calculating Total Income

It is relatively easy for them to work out their total income for the year; it is simply their wages plus the rents from the two properties. So total income will be $61,640 ($40,000 + $5,000 + $8,320 + $8,320).

Calculating Total Expenditure

Working out the total expenditure for the year is not quite as straight forward. Expenditure includes their tax liability, rental property expenses, interest on the loan and their living expenses. If both the properties are in the husband's name, their tax liability would be greatly reduced because of negative gearing. Let's look at these tax benefits first (see chapters 15, 16 and the Appendix for more detail on tax calculations).

Tax Benefits for One Rental Property

Interest	$14,630
Property Expenses (20% of Rent)	+ $1,664
Non-Cash Deductions	+ $4,300
Total Deductions	$20,594
Rent	− $8,320
Tax Loss	$12,274
Tax Refund (Tax on $40,000) − (Tax on $27,726)	$5,138

For each property, the total deductions are $20,594, made up of interest on the loan ($14,630), property expenses (20% of gross rent, or $1,664) and non-cash deductions (depreciation and loan costs etc of say $4,300). After subtracting the rent of $8,320, the tax loss on each property is then $12,274. For the first property, this loss would reduce the taxable income from $40,000 to $27,726 resulting in a tax refund of $5,138. For the second property, the tax refund of $3,862, is less than the first because the calculations are now based on the reduced taxable income of $27,726.

One of the most important aspects of the tax refund for any income earner is that a variation of tax (under Section 221D) can be obtained from the Taxation Office so that the tax benefit is obtained progressively. In this respect, the tax refund can be considered as a tax credit that is simply subtracted from the tax to be paid through the PAYE system.

With total tax credits at $9,000 ($5,138 + $3,862), the husband's tax liability would reduce to $2,250 ($11,250 – $9,000). So total expenditure for the first year would be $50,338, made up of living expenses ($15,500), interest on the loans ($29,260), property expenses ($3,328) and tax liability ($2,250). From this, you can see that this couple still have an excess of $11,302 ($61,640 – $50,338), even with the two investment properties. Let's combine the two parts of the budget.

Budget for First Year

INCOME		EXPENDITURE	
Husband's Income	$40,000	Husband's Tax ($11,250 – $9,000)	$2,250
Wife's Income	$5,000	Wife's Tax	$0
Rent Prop. A	$8,320	Expenses Prop. A	$1,664
		Interest Prop. A	$14,630
Rent Prop. B	$8,320	Expenses Prop. B	$1,664
		Interest Prop. B	$14,630
		Living Expenses	$15,500
TOTAL IN	$61,640	TOTAL OUT	$50,338
EXCESS = Total Income – Total Expenditure = $11,302			

Now that you can see how to budget, let's look at what happens over the next 10 years so that some of the "how" and "when" questions can be answered. Over time, wages go up, rents rise, living expenses increase and of course, property grows in value. The table below shows you the rates of increase that I will use in the projections over 10 years.

Yearly Rates of Increase Used in Projections

	30 Year Averages	Rates
Wages	9.7%	9.5%
Rent	9.2%	8.0%
Living Expenses	8.0%	8.0%
Property Values	10% to 12%	11.0%

It is important to note that I am using more than achievable figures and that I've deliberately avoided using unrealistic increases in values. However, although there can be no guarantees of future performance, I think that using the averages for the past 30 years is a good starting point on which to base future estimates. Consequently, the yearly increases I have used are equal to, or less than, these 30 year Australian averages.

Using these increases, we produced a table (next page) that shows you progressively how everything gradually increases with time and the young couple can then go on to buy a rental property every two years. The chart accompanying the table gives you a graphic picture of how this wealth building is achieved.

In the beginning, our hypothetical couple have an excess (savings) in the first year of $11,302. After one year, their salary and rent increase with inflation, while the interest remains fixed. With a good history of loan repayments, they buy their third rental property, for which they must pay the increased price (due to growth) of $111,000. Their net worth has now increased to $119,005 or, if we exclude their home, $8,005.

By the end of year three, salary and rents increase to the extent that they can buy their fourth rental property at the increased price of $136,763. They still have an excess of money that they can either spend or save. With time, rents, salary and property values increase and after 10 years, they would have 7 investment properties with a total value of $2,271,537 and debt of $1,128,275. *This would give them a net worth of more than one million dollars, or $859,320 without their own home.*

What do they do after 10 years? If they continued buying, borrowing and keeping property for just another 5 years while they worked, their net worth would be almost three million dollars! By then they would have 10 rental properties and the sale of 5 would completely clear the debt. This would give them direct income of rent from the remaining five properties, which would be the equivalent in today's dollars to $33,000 per year net, and they could retire completely!

They may decide to work part-time at half salary and not buy any more properties. Then the sale of two properties after 10 years would reduce the debt, such that the rent and tax savings would balance the interest. After working part-time for 7 years, the sale of just one property should clear the remaining debt, giving them four properties outright and a net income (equivalent in today's dollars) of almost $27,000.

Wouldn't you like to set a goal similar to this young couple? You can you know! And no matter what your circumstance, I believe that building wealth through investment property will give you a much wealthier and earlier retirement than would otherwise be possible.

Building Wealth Through Investment Property By Buying One Property Every Two Years

Year	0	1	2	3	4	5	6	7	8	9	10
1 Joint Income	45,000	49,275	53,956	59,082	64,695	70,841	77,571	84,940	93,009	101,845	111,520
2 Tax	11,250	12,319	13,489	14,770	16,174	17,710	19,393	21,235	23,252	25,461	27,880
Tax Refund	9,000	9,855	10,791	11,816	12,939	14,168	15,514	16,988	18,602	20,369	22,304
Tax Payable	2,250	2,464	2,698	2,954	3,235	3,542	3,879	4,247	4,650	5,092	5,576
3 Rent per Property	8,320	8,986	9,704	10,481	11,319	12,225	13,203	14,259	15,400	16,632	17,962
Gross Rent	16,640	26,957	29,113	41,923	45,277	61,124	66,014	85,554	92,398	116,422	125,736
Property Exp.	3,328	5,391	5,823	8,385	9,055	12,225	13,203	17,111	18,480	23,284	25,147
4 Total Income	61,640	76,232	83,069	101,005	109,972	131,965	143,585	170,494	185,408	218,267	237,256
5 Interest	29,260	45,499	45,499	65,508	65,508	90,160	90,160	120,534	120,534	157,958	157,958
6 Living Exp.	15,500	16,740	18,079	19,526	21,088	22,775	24,597	26,564	28,689	30,985	33,463
7 Total Expenditure	50,338	70,094	72,099	96,372	98,885	128,702	131,838	168,456	172,354	217,320	222,145
8 Excess	11,302	6,137	10,970	4,633	11,086	3,263	11,747	2,037	13,054	947	15,111
9 Amount Invested	6,948	14,079	11,417	20,153	16,347	27,093	21,835	35,103	28,014	44,452	35,066
10 Property Value	100,000	111,000	123,210	136,763	151,807	168,506	187,041	207,616	230,454	255,804	283,942
Total Property	300,000	444,000	492,840	683,816	759,035	1,011,035	1,122,249	1,453,312	1,613,176	2,046,430	2,271,537
Inv. Properties	2	3	3	4	4	5	5	6	6	7	7
11 Loans	209,000	324,995	324,995	467,912	467,912	644,001	644,001	860,960	860,960	1,128,275	1,128,275
12 Networth	91,000	119,005	167,845	215,903	291,123	367,034	478,248	592,352	752,217	918,155	1,143,262
Netwth-Home	-9,000	8,005	44,635	79,140	139,316	198,528	291,206	384,736	521,763	662,351	859,320

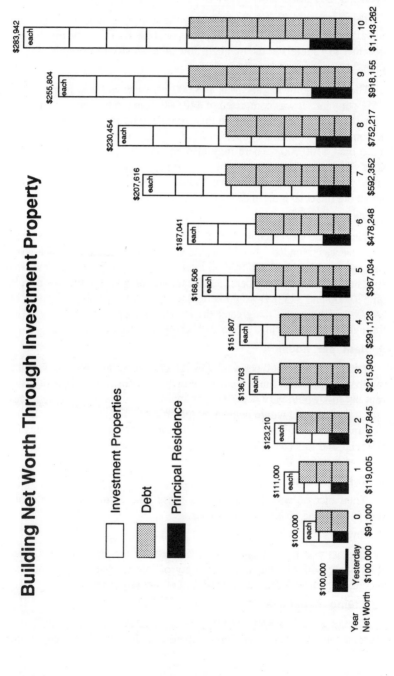

Building Net Worth Through Investment Property

Notes on Building Wealth Table

The following notes explain the way the preceding table was tabulated and also discusses the possible variations on these figures. The numbering system 1 to 12 refers to the numbers down the left side of the table.

1. Joint income

The initial joint income was $45,000 per year and was increased at 9.5% per year. It was comprised of $40,000 from the husband and $5,000 from the wife. The variations on this are numerous and may range from a person on $20,000, to a couple on $25,000 each, to company incomes of more than $100,000. There may also be two incomes for a few years, after which the woman leaves the workforce to have a family, but rejoins later. But you need to realise that high incomes are not a prerequisite for achieving financial independence in 10 to 15 years.

2. Tax

The tax due was calculated at 25% of the wage and it was also assumed that 80% was refunded – but this would vary with the deductions each year. The tax would depend not only on total income, but how the income was split between family members. For example, the total tax for two people on $20,000 and $25,000 would be less than the tax on a single income of $45,000. Obviously, the greater the income, the greater the tax benefits through negative gearing, but anyone who pays tax can still benefit.

3. Rent per house

Initial rent was $160 per week ($8,320 per year) and gross rent was the number of properties times the rent. Property expenses were 20% of gross rent but this would vary depending on maintenance and management fees etc. The rent level would depend on the property and the location. In the example, rents were increased at 8% per year – however, increases may be irregular and this can affect the future rate of property purchase more so than the increases in property values.

4. Total income

Total income was the sum of the gross joint income plus the gross rent from all the investment properties.

5. Interest

Interest was interest-only and 14% fixed for the 10 years. It's more than likely you will encounter a variety of interest rates throughout the process, which will affect the rate of further property purchases.

6. Living expenses

Living expenses were initially set at $15,500 per year and were increased at 8.0% per year. These expenses include the day to day living costs such as food, clothes, car costs, petrol, phone, electricity, holidays and any other interest payments such as car loans or existing mortgages. And herein lies the crux of the matter! The amount you spend on normal living costs is a prime factor in determining just how fast you build your wealth – a few years of frugality ensures many years of prosperity.

7. Total expenditure

Total expenditure was the sum of the tax payable, property expenses, interest on the loan and living expenses.

8. The excess

The excess was total income less total expenditure. It is the cue to when the next property is affordable because with natural increases in rent and salary, this excess increases to the point where another property can be purchased. The excess is then reduced that year accordingly. What you do with this money is entirely up to you. It can be saved or spent or it can be used from one year to the next to balance any negative cash flow. It is simply a figure to show you that the given situation is possible.

9. Amount invested

The amount invested was interest less net rent and tax credit. It is the after-tax cash flow from the properties, or your contribution to the system. Later in this chapter, I have made a comparison to show you just how much or how little you would have achieved if you had contributed the same sum to either a superannuation fund or a bank deposit.

10. Property value

The value of the principal place of residence and first two investment properties was initially $100,000 each but this will be one of the greatest variants of all the figures used. The total property value is the sum of all the properties, including the principal place of residence. But this could well be made up of 10 cheaper properties or 4 dearer properties, depending on your area. The property value was increased each year at 11%.

11. Loans

Loans are the total of existing loans plus any new loans. All loans include borrowing and purchasing costs (4.5% of the property value). So each property is bought with a loan that is 104.5% of the property value.

12. Net worth

Net worth may or may not include the principal place of residence. By the tenth year, there are seven rental properties plus the principal place of residence, making a total of eight. At this stage, net worth, including the principal residence, has surpassed one million dollars. Over the 10 years, net worth has roughly doubled every three years.

Comparing Wealth from Property, Superannuation and Cash

Now that you've seen what property investment can do for you, we should put it in perspective and look at what is possible by putting the same amount of money towards superannuation or by depositing it in the bank (see figure opposite). The contributions (the amount invested from row 9 of previous table) were used to calculate the result if the money had been invested in each of these areas – cash, superannuation and property. To make fair comparisons, the marginal tax rate of 39.25% (38% + 1.25% Medicare) and growth rate at 11%, have been used in all situations.

The bank equivalent allows for the contribution to be deposited in a bank account earning 11% and taxed at 39.25%, with interest redeposited at the end of each year.

The superannuation equivalent is calculated by investing contributions into a superannuation fund where the growth was 11%. After allowing for the 15% tax on fund earnings, real growth was calculated at 9.5%. For legitimate comparison to property, it was assumed that the tax refunds resulting from the superannuation contribution were reinvested into the fund. Tax credits were calculated at the marginal tax rate of 39.25% and on the basis that the first $3,000 and 75% of the remaining contributions were tax deductible. With the superannuation calculations, initial set up costs have not been taken into account.

The "money" from property is the equity build up over the 10 year period with capital growth at 11%. Contributions (from row 9) are based on the difference between the interest, rent and tax refund. ALL costs, including setup costs, were accounted for – hence the initial $9,000 deficit that produced an initial negative net worth.

You can see from the figure that property as an investment, has the ability to outperform either superannuation or term deposits. After 10 years in property, it is possible to achieve more than twice the amount built up in a super fund – or, in this case, roughly $500,000 more! And with time, the gap widens further. This means that through investment in property, it is possible to enjoy a much earlier and wealthier retirement.

As I've stated all along, there's nothing wrong with a normal superannuation fund if all you want is to stave off the pension. However, I believe that today's superannuation is tomorrow's pension, and unless you do something instead of, or as well as superannuation, you will never become financially independent. And as for money invested in the bank, it does not even compare with superannuation, let alone property!

As a vehicle for building wealth, residential property is outstanding!

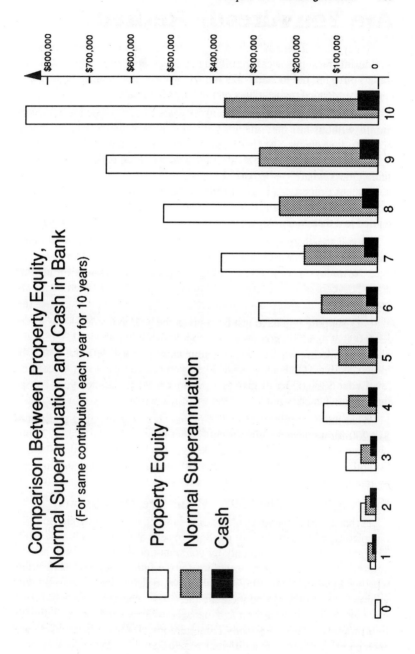

Comparison Between Property Equity, Normal Superannuation and Cash in Bank

(For same contribution each year for 10 years)

Property Equity

Normal Superannuation

Cash

Are You Already Retired?

Have you just retired with a large superannuation payout? Are you wondering how this wealth building strategy applies to you? Do you think you're too old to start? Let me tell you about a "young" couple who regularly attended my seminars on the Sunshine Coast.

Fred and Mary are about 77 and 75 years of age respectively. Every month without fail they attended the seminars at which I spoke about property investment. At first I thought they were there for the evening's entertainment until one night, after the seminar, Fred called me aside and said "Guess what?" – "What?" I replied. He answered "I've bought an investment property." I was a little taken back, for then I realised they were there for more than a little social interaction. "Good on you Fred," I replied and then Mary chimed in with – "Yes, it's for when we get old!!!"

So you see, there is no age limit to start investing in property and Fred and Mary were obviously looking forward to a long life ahead, despite their age. Nowadays, people retiring at age 55 should be planning for another 20 to 30 years of active life. And the sooner you start to plan for it, the better.

Let's suppose you have just been given the golden handshake of a cool $300,000 at age 55. You own your own home worth about $150,000 and you're wondering what to do with your money. First, let's put $300,000 in perspective. Go back to page 23 so you can see what sort of comfort level your $300,000 will give you. I don't want to dampen your spirits, but it doesn't exactly put you in the wealthy category.

What many people don't realise is that receiving the aged pension of $13,200 for a married couple is equivalent to having more than $220,000 invested, providing 6% income and 8% growth (to keep up with inflation). So with your $300,000, you're better off than an aged pensioner, but not by much. Let's see what you can do with your money.

Retiring with $300,000?   What are the options?

Perhaps the most important decision is whether you are going to retire completely, work part-time, or continue to seek alternative full-time work. This may be influenced not only by your emotional preference but also by your financial needs and expectations for the future. As well as deciding whether to work or not, you will still have to determine what to do with your money. You will find there are three basic choices: you could put it into a bank deposit, transfer it to a managed rollover fund, or put it directly into property. There are many combinations of what you could do and each person will arrive at a different conclusion. Let's take a look at a few of these many options.

Option 1: Put it in the bank and stop work altogether.

When someone who has worked all their lives suddenly finds themselves with a few hundred thousand dollars, they feel rich. You would probably feel exactly the same way. You've probably never had so much money before and the chances are you will want to take more control. If you do take control, the obvious option is to get hold of the money and put it straight into a bank deposit where it is "secure". If you do some mental arithmetic, 10% interest on $300,000 would give you a nice income of $30,000 a year, which is probably almost as much as you were earning before you retired.

But just hold on a minute. Don't forget about paying tax on your money and don't forget about inflation! Even if you split the income with your wife, you will still pay tax of around $5,000 per year. The residual $25,000 may still sound like an awful lot of money but let's look at what inflation will do to it. Take a look back to page 22 where I showed you that $200,000 would last just 9 years if you spend it at less than the basic wage! Well $300,000 won't last much longer – in fact, just over 13 years.

Living costs will continue to rise (see chapter 3 to remind yourself of the 8% inflation we have experienced over the last 30 years) and after a few short years, your $30,000 per year won't sound wealthy anymore. And since the life expectancy of the average Australian is close to 80 years of age, you should be thinking now what you are going to do with the rest of your life when the money runs out. Maybe this option suits some people – live it up for the next ten years, fall back on the aged pension (if there is one) and leave nothing for the kids. I think that most people really don't want to let this happen, but unfortunately it does happen and by the time people realise it has happened, it is too late to do anything about it.

Option 2: Put it in a rollover fund and continue to work.

You could simply move the money into a rollover fund where the tax advantages are similar to superannuation and then continue to work. This has the effect of deferring any real decision until you are 65. If you do decide to take this option, I suggest you talk to a competent independent financial advisor about the best placement of your funds. If you are self-employed, there is a real possibility that you could buy rental property in the name of your superannuation fund and continue to receive the tax advantages on the rent. You should check with your accountant about this possibility. If you decide to continue working full time, you could then consider embarking on a wealth building plan as outlined throughout this book and borrow to buy rental properties. You should then receive all the negative gearing advantages while you are working and when you retire eventually, you could use your rollover payout to reduce the debt.

Option 3: Put it into property and work part-time.

Let's suppose you decide to accept the superannuation payout and put your money directly into rental property. And because you're active, and you want to continue enjoying a good lifestyle, you also take a part-time job earning around $10,000 per year. There are many options available to you then, but one option could look like this.

- Put $40,000 of your $300,000 aside in a term deposit or bank account as a security factor and re-invest the interest.

- With your remaining $260,000, you could borrow a small amount of around $50,000 giving you a total of $310,000 with which to buy property (over the years, banks have changed their views on lending to older people). Why put money in the bank and then borrow more? I believe it is better to borrow and have cash on hand as a safety factor, rather than investing the entire amount into property.

- With your $310,000 you could buy either two properties for $150,000 or three for $100,000 with $10,000 purchasing and borrowing costs. If we assume three properties are bought and then rented for $160 each ($8,320 per year), this would give you a net income of about $6,000 per property (after property expenses including a property manager).

- Your total income would be $18,000 (3 times $6,000 net rent) less the interest of $7,000 (14% of $50,000 borrowed) giving you $11,000 per year clear. If you re-invest the interest from the $40,000 deposit rather than spend it, then $11,000 would be your total income from your investments.

- Now more than likely, an income of $11,000 is not enough, so if you worked part-time for an additional $10,000 per year, this would give you a total income of $21,000 (less $2,000 tax). Not only would it add to your coffers, but it would also greatly add to your enjoyment by maintaining social interaction and providing mental stimulation. And you would still have time to do the things you always wanted to do.

- What's the situation after 10 years? If capital growth was 11% over 10 years, your three properties should be worth more than $280,000 each and you could clear the $50,000 debt with some of the cash in the bank. Or you could even consider selling a property to not only clear the debt, but buy a new car, have an overseas holiday, or give something to the children. Your rents should have risen with inflation to more than $39,000 net ($18,000 in today's dollars or $16,000 after tax), and you could probably have afforded to have given up your part-time job well before this. Furthermore, rents and property values should continue to rise, giving you an inflation-proofed retirement.

When you retire with a seemingly wealthy amount of $300,000, you must look realistically into the future. You have already seen that money in the bank does not allow your money to grow, and while the income seems great, the capital base is not keeping pace with inflation. This provides you with a short-term solution, however, with medical advances enabling longer life expectancies, you should be looking longer term.

But no matter what path you follow, a large chunk of your money must be directed into areas of capital growth. This means that if you want to continue enjoying a good lifestyle, *and* secure your financial future, you may find it necessary to continue working, at least at a part-time level.

If you prefer to leave your funds in a managed environment, then as I pointed out in chapter 5, you pay the price and you relinquish control to someone else. However, I believe income-producing property can satisfy all the criteria for a long and prosperous retirement. With its high and consistent capital growth and rents rising with inflation, it can provide one of the best mechanisms for not only building wealth, but preserving wealth. Your nest egg needs to be *inflation-proofed* and what better way than through property.

PART IV

The Tools
for Building
Wealth

11
Clever Use
of Collateral

One of the greatest attributes of property is its value as collateral or security for loans. Security or collateral, is a financier's guarantee that you will repay the money. As I've already pointed out, financial institutions regard residential property as such a sound, secure investment, that they are willing to lend up to 90% of the value of the property. Usually this is by way of a mortgage on the property but, in many cases, insurance bonds may be used as security for a loan.

It is this borrowing capacity that provides you with a continual source of finance to plough into property investment, without having to put up any cash deposits of your own. Once you have built up a considerable amount of wealth through investment in property, you'll find that you'll only be limited by your capacity to service the loans, not by how much property you're capable of mortgaging. In theory, if you own property worth $100,000, you should be able to borrow $900,000 for investment property. In practice, you'll be limited to a few hundred thousand dollars because you need to be able to service the loan.

A caller on a radio talk-back show I was doing some time ago posed a very simple question about borrowing money. He and his wife had a joint income of around $60,000 per year and a mortgage of just $25,000 on their $250,000 home. This couple's existing mortgage was with a large Australian Bank where the owner-occupied rate was OK, but the property investment rate was higher than that for other institutions. His question was "How do we borrow money to buy a $140,000 rental property, and still buy more later?" The brief answer I gave, because of time limitations, was simply, "Borrow against your own property to buy the rental property, and when they both go up in value, borrow to buy more."

But I think it a most useful exercise to examine all the possible ways to do this, so that you can see that there's more to borrowing money than just mortgaging property. In fact, I spend more time considering how to organise the finances than looking for a property.

- One option would be to refinance the first mortgage with the same institution and borrow an additional $150,000 to cover purchase price, purchase and borrowing costs and a little extra. In this instance, they should keep the two loans separate so that they could continue paying out the first loan, but not the second investment loan. The second property would then be free of a mortgage (unencumbered) and could be mortgaged for a second investment property at some future date.

- Alternatively, they could go to another financial institution and offer a second mortgage on their home and a first mortgage on their investment property. But this could limit their next step of buying more property, because *both* the properties are then "tied up" – or encumbered.

- Yet another alternative would be to approach a different institution to refinance their existing home loan so that the two loans of $25,000 and $150,000 would be with the one, but different institution. It can be costly to change the first mortgage over, but it may be advantageous if the investment loan interest rate is much lower. But again, the two loans must be kept separate so that it is clear which is for investment purposes, and which is not.

- A further option would be to use an equity-access type of loan (one that can be continually drawn on and repaid like a cheque account) with the first bank on their own home. This allows them to continually draw down enough deposit for any property and to finance the remainder through a different institution. The problem with this would be that the initial home loan would get tangled up with the "access" loan and its identity lost. This makes paying back the home loan very difficult.

- A variation on the "access" loan would be to take a "second mortgage access" loan over and above the existing home loan. This would still allow money to be drawn down for a deposit on the rental property and repaid at will, however the interest rate is likely to be higher. The advantage would be that the home loan could be kept separate and also that the money drawn down as a deposit would enable yet another financial institution to finance the rental property.

As you can see, there are many ways to solve this problem and these few options should give you plenty of food for thought. Don't leave it to the bank to decide how to arrange your finance. They'll choose the option that is easiest for them but not necessarily best for you and furthermore, they will take as much security as they can possibly get. It's not un-common to find people with loans of around $15,000, where the bank is holding properties worth several hundred thousand dollars as security!

Creative use of mortgages can greatly improve the returns from your property investment portfolio, and allow you to be less restricted in your wealth building plans. It's most important to realise that you don't need large amounts of cash upfront to invest in property and there's always more than one way to finance or refinance property. The manner in which your assets are used as collateral is just as important as where you borrow money and this becomes more important after you've purchased three or four properties.

If you have not set up your finance appropriately early on, it may prove costly to rearrange later because of all the re-setup charges that could amount to several thousand dollars. Whenever I am about to purchase property, I may spend several weeks sorting through the options available to me to finance the property, and several days looking for the property. Be flexible, think laterally and consider the following points before you mortgage anything to buy more property.

Deposits

Cash deposits are not necessary if other collateral can be used as cross-collateralisation. For example, if you own your own home, you can use this as security for your next rental property. There is no need to "save up a deposit" for that next property. Saving for a deposit of between 5% to 30% and borrowing the rest may be the time-honoured method of buying your first home but it is not necessarily the best way to acquire investment property. Saving for a deposit means that for every dollar you earn, you give almost half back in tax, and if the remaining money is invested in the bank, more tax must be paid on the interest you earn. So for every step forward, you go two steps back. It can take a very long time to save for a deposit at this rate and by the time you have enough for a deposit, property values have increased.

Loan size

When other properties are available as collateral for the loan, it may be possible to borrow the entire purchase price, the purchasing and borrowing costs and some extra cash as a reserve. You can even borrow enough for the deposit on the next house or to prepay the interest upfront. And don't forget about any renovation costs, rates, insurances or management fees. The list is unlimited.

Providing you have the capacity to service the loan, the financial institution will usually lend you any amount you wish for your rental property. There are, however, some financial institutions such as the building societies, that may restrict loans to the purchase price only. But no matter how much you borrow, the onus is on you to justify to the Tax Office why you borrowed the money. It all boils down to the purpose of the loan (see below). As an example, for a $130,000 property, you might seek a loan to cover the following:

Purchase price	$130,000
Purchase costs	$3,500
Borrowing costs	$3,500
Cash reserve	$13,000
Deposit on next property	$15,000
First year's interest prepaid	$30,000
Renovation costs	$5,000
TOTAL LOAN	**$200,000**

Purpose of the loan

For tax purposes, it is not the asset *mortgaged* that is relevant, but the *purpose* of the loan. It is possible for the interest on a loan against your principal place of residence to be tax deductible. Normally, this is not the case if the loan is used to buy your own home. However, if the funds are used to purchase income-producing investment property, then the interest would be tax deductible. As distinct from this, you cannot use money borrowed against a rental property to buy a new kitchen for your own home, and still expect the interest to be tax deductible.

This distinction is very important when people who own their own home, decide to go upmarket to their dream home. Many will decide to keep their existing home for investment (because they have seen just how good an investment it has been), and borrow against it to build their new house. They then have an investment property with a mortgage – but the loan is not tax deductible, because the purpose of the loan was to build their new house and not to buy the rental property.

A solution would be to sell the first home, put the proceeds towards the new house and borrow against this new house to buy a rental property. Their principal place of residence would now be mortgaged, but the actual purpose of the loan would be to buy a rental property. The interest on the loan in this case would be fully tax deductible.

However, although selling their first home would be the best solution, it may not be necessary to sell to a "third party" – i.e. an outsider. It may be possible (depending on ownership), to sell from wife to husband or vice versa. If the property is jointly owned, selling half the property to one or the other may provide a part answer.

Change of ownership in this manner means paying stamp duty and legals, but the tax benefits may far outweigh the costs. A few thousand dollars in stamp duty could be recouped many times over in just a couple of years through tax saved. Check with your accountant first, though, before you attempt any within family transactions.

Name on the title

Properties with a negative cash flow should be bought in the name of the highest-income earner, while property bought with a positive cash flow, should be bought in the name of the lowest-income earner. You should also check with your accountant to ascertain if the property should be in joint names, and if so, whether as Tenants in Common or as Joint Tenants. As Tenants in Common, it is usually easier to apportion unequal percentages in ownership and it may also be possible to nominate the equity/debt sharing arrangements in such a partnership (e.g. one owner could pay cash for their share, receive income and pay tax, while the other could service a loan and possibly receive tax benefits).

Properties bought in a company name warrant special mention. In most cases, if you borrow to buy rental property, it is best bought in an individual's name. However, many people wrongly assume that company and trust structures confer greater tax benefits. First, the company tax rate of 39% is less than the top personal rate of 47%. Secondly, on the sale of the property, while the capital gains are inflation-indexed before assessing company tax, when distributed to the shareholders, these gains are taxed at their full marginal tax rate, without allowance for inflation. Even gains that are less than inflation may be taxed in this way. If you must borrow substantially for your principal residence, buying it in your company's name and renting it back may reduce your company's tax burden. However, your property may then be liable for capital gains tax.

Borrowing to buy property through trusts can nullify any negative gearing benefits unless the trust is earning a large income from other sources. However, capital gains can be better distributed through trusts than through companies. Properties bought by family trusts do provide tax advantages if there is income to be distributed. Consequently, trusts are usually only useful when you have retired and wish to utilise the profits in a tax effective manner.

Name on the mortgage

For many couples, the lending institution will require both names on a mortgage document, even though the title to the property is in the name of the husband only. However, this is not a problem because it is more important to have the correct name on the property title than on the loan document. In effect, the financier has lent half the money to the wife, who then lent it to the husband. She gets interest from her husband and pays it to the financier, so her tax position is neutral.

Unencumbered property

An unencumbered property is one that it is not mortgaged. For tax purposes, there may be a loan on it (mortgaged to another property), but it is free to be mortgaged for further property acquisition. For example, if your principal place of residence is valued at $150,000 and mortgaged for $100,000 to purchase a rental property for $95,000 (with an additional $5,000 for costs), the rental property has not been mortgaged and is thus unencumbered. However, your principal place of residence is encumbered (mortgaged), but the purpose of the loan was for the rental property – the interest on the loan is therefore tax-deductible. Try to keep at least one of your properties unencumbered to maintain a degree of flexibility, though this may be difficult in the early stages of building a property portfolio.

Loan to value ratio

The loan to value ratio (L/V ratio) is the loan divided by the value of the property mortgaged. Although many banks will lend to about 90% of the value of property, don't confuse this with the fact that you can borrow the total purchase price if you use other security. It is the total value of the properties being *mortgaged* that is used in calculating the L/V ratio, not the property being *purchased*. For example, if you own your own home worth $100,000 and you wish to purchase two more properties worth $100,000 each, you could mortgage all the properties for a total value of $300,000. Against this you could borrow $200,000 for the two extra properties, $10,000 for the purchasing and borrowing costs and $10,000 for additional cash flow throughout the year making a total of $220,000. This is a loan to value ratio of 73% ($220,000/$300,000) – or, an asset:debt ratio of roughly 3:2.

But be careful. Some financial institutions will not lend more than 80% of *their* valuation, which in turn may only be 80% of true *market* value. This would result in an L/V ratio on one property alone of 64%! On the other hand, some will go as high as 95%. It's important to know how much you can borrow on a property, as it may be better to forego a low interest rate offered by a company who only lend to 60%, in favour of a slightly higher interest rate where the maximum L/V ratio is 95% of market value. It's a good idea to get maximum mileage from L/V ratios so that you mortgage the least amount of property for the maximum amount of loan. In other words, don't give the financial institution any more security than they need. This enables you to keep future investment options open by having as many unencumbered properties as possible.

Also be wary when you are refinancing properties and they are revalued by valuers contracted by financial institutions. Values rarely come up to your expectations, partly because you tend to overvalue your property and partly because valuers are understandably conservative. This can result in either a lower loan than anticipated, a higher rate of mortgage insurance, or giving the financier more property to mortgage.

Penalty clauses

It is almost impossible to decipher many of the clauses in mortgage documents, but you should at least take the time to find out about the penalties for early loan repayment. These penalties can be prohibitive and can be up to four months interest. Alternatively, the penalty may be that you have to pay the difference between the going market rate of interest, and what you are paying now, for the remaining term of the loan. This may prevent you from refinancing the way you want and can delay your purchase of more property. Normally, if you are keeping property long-term, these penalties are acceptable, but it is better to be wise in foresight than hindsight.

Substitution of collateral

Substituting one property for another on a mortgage document is called substitution of collateral. It could be costly if you want to sell a property or refinance it when there is no provision for substituting another property as security on the mortgage document. Usually, the cost is only small.

Assumable loans

An assumable loan is one that can be "tied" to the property, even if it is sold. In other words, you can sell the property together with the terms of the mortgage and it usually only requires a simple change in owner's name. This can be handy, should you wish to sell, if there is a very low interest rate attached to the mortgage with a few years left on the term. It can also be worth a lot if you manage to buy a property with an assumable loan, particularly if the interest rate attached to the loan is low. However, very few loans in Australia are assumable.

Second mortgages

The idea of a second mortgage is foreign to most people because it is usually associated with "being on the brink of insolvency". However, this is not necessarily the case. Second mortgages can be less expensive than paying mortgage insurance and the interest rate is often the same as a first mortgage. If you are lucky enough to have an old War Service loan at 5%, and want to borrow more for a rental property, don't refinance the loan by giving another financial institution a first mortgage. It might be cheaper to borrow a small amount on second mortgage, even at 20%.

Multi-property mortgages

Don't tie up more than two or three properties on the one mortgage document, as it may be costly to release a particular property from the mortgage. It is slightly more expensive to request individual mortgages on individual properties but it may save you a lot of time and expense in the future should you wish to do something with a particular property.

Deed of variation of loan

When property values rise, you could consider a "deed of variation of loan". This involves having the properties revalued so that you can then borrow against the increased equity to buy more property on the same mortgage. You may be up for valuation and solicitor's fees, but you should only have to pay stamp duty on the amount of loan variation.

Cash contracts

A cash contract means that the purchase of a property is not subject to finance. There may be finance involved, but the purchaser has "teed up " the finance beforehand. You can use other property, or the prospective property, as security to have finance pre-approved, or you can simply use cash. Cash contracts are attractive to vendors and they can help you gain an advantage with respect to the price. Signing a contract "subject to finance" in the hope that it is a way out is not a sound arrangement in today's financial world, as finance is relatively easy to obtain.

Cheque-book mortgages

"Cheque-book" mortgages are loans that enable you to use collateral as security for a cheque-book facility. They go by a variety of names such as mortgage power, smarter mortgage, mortgage manager, and equity access loans, to name but a few. The bank takes a mortgage over your property and gives you a credit facility that you can draw against and repay at your discretion. The loans work like an overdraft with an upper limit, but you only pay interest on the balance outstanding at any point in time.

They have a number of uses and I strongly recommend that once you have a few properties, you should set one of these loans in place. They can be used to pay a deposit on another property, to pay the interest bills, or to pay the tax bills. These types of loans are also good as an instant source of cash for picking up "bargains" through cash contracts, but they are not so great for long-term property investments as the interest rates tend to be higher. What you can do is buy the property with your cheque-book loan and then refinance to a less expensive, less flexible, fixed-interest loan at your leisure.

I find these loans an invaluable source of overdraft money for business and as a substitute for having ready cash if needed for the rental properties. Building wealth through investment property requires you to have a ready source of credit as a backup. However you needn't have cash sitting in bank deposits. A credit line in the form of a "cheque-book" mortgage can be just as effective and much cheaper.

12
Costs of Finance

There is more to consider than just interest rates when you are working out the real cost of financing an investment property. In fact, simple comparisons between the interest rates offered by the various financial institutions can not only be confusing, but downright misleading.

A few years ago, when interest rates for property were around 16.5%, a friend rang me and asked what I thought about taking loan money at an interest rate of 12.5%. It sounded too good to be true, he said. My instant reaction was that there is no such thing as a free lunch and so I gave my friend a list of questions to ask the financier about any other less obvious borrowing costs.

Sure enough, in the midst of a whole host of "other charges", was an establishment fee of 3%, mortgagee's solicitors charges of $2,500, and compulsory mortgage insurance, all of which suddenly made the loan much less attractive. In fact, the effective rate of interest over 3 years was 17%! Now this was a fairly exceptional case, but it proves the point that there is more to interest rates than meets the eye.

Many investors go to great lengths to ensure that they purchase an investment property at bargain basement prices. They spend many months agonising and haggling over prices, and travel hundreds of kilometres looking at properties. Yet when it comes to financing the property, they might spend a few hours one afternoon deciding where to borrow the money. Optimal financing can far outweigh the apparent gains of buying property at bargain prices.

However, don't do a "ring around" of all the financial institutions and simply ask for the current interest rate – it's really quite meaningless. I'm sure you wouldn't dream of ringing up your local electrical shop to ask for the price of just any TV. To get a fair comparison between the shops, you'd need to find out about the size, style, warranty and all the other relevant features. "Buying" money is no different. You need information about both the interest rate and the upfront costs before the real cost of borrowing becomes apparent.

Interest Costs

Interest is the "rent" you pay on borrowed money and is an ongoing cost. But there are so many different ways of calculating interest that you might be comparing apples with oranges. Below are some of the factors you need to consider about interest.

Is the interest rate fixed or variable?

Interest rates can be fixed for varying periods from as little as 90 days, to as long as 10 years or more. Whether you decide to take a variable or fixed rate depends on your perception of the money market (something on which even economists can't agree) and your financial muscle (i.e. can your budget withstand an upward movement in interest rates).

Fixed-interest loans can be very useful if you're buying long-term and I strongly recommend them. Cash flow budgets are important to property investors and fixed interest rates allow for better budgeting and peace of mind. Some of the fixed rates of interest I have are as high as 16.4%, while others are as low as 11.6%. If interest rates go up, I'm protected. If they go down, I still manage to smile. Usually the lowering of interest rates is followed by a rush on housing with subsequent price increases that ultimately add to my net worth.

Usually, three years is a desirable term to fix the interest, however if you come across a particularly attractive rate, it may be worthwhile fixing the rate for a longer term. As you might expect, three-year fixed interest rates are more stable than either variable rates or short-term bank bills, as indicated by the figures over the last 10 years, shown below.

1982 – 1992 Property Investment Loan Rates

Fixed 3-year rates	11 – 17%
Variable rates	9 – 19%
90-day bank bills	8 – 21%

Is the loan principal and interest, or interest-only?

A principal and interest (P & I) loan requires part of the principal to be paid back as well as the interest, usually each month, so that at the end of the term of the loan, it is completely paid out. An interest-only (IO) loan requires only the interest to be paid during the term of the loan (again usually each month) with the principal being paid back in full (or more usually refinanced) at the end of the term.

Interest-only loans are the best for financing rental property but too many bank managers suggest short-term P & I loans to clients, without explaining to them the important taxation implications, and the drain it places on their budget.

The main disadvantages of a principal & interest loan are:

- The part of the repayment towards the principal is not tax deductible.
- Because the principal is reducing, the amount of interest also reduces. This reduces the total claims against rent, and you lose tax benefits.
- The larger monthly repayment reduces your ability to fund further properties.
- The principal repayment is from after-tax dollars. So, to pay $1,000 towards the principal, you might need to earn around $2,000.

Interest-only loans maximise your cash flow and allow you to service the loans on more properties. With an interest-only loan, there is always a loan on the property which, although constant in amount, is declining in terms of the dollar value. Your net worth can build up by normal capital growth much faster by paying interest-only on several properties, than by paying back the principal and building up equity in just one.

Consider if you had bought a property 15 years ago for $23,000 and borrowed the entire amount of money as an interest-only loan. At all times your name is on the title to the property, despite the fact that you have a "never-ending" loan. If you borrowed the $23,000 as an interest-only loan, then today you would still owe that same $23,000, but the property would probably be worth around $110,000. The loan is still in "yesterday's" dollars, while the property increases in value in "today's" dollars. The equity build up should be your ultimate aim. As well as this, the rent should have overtaken the interest payment, so that in time, the property should produce a positive cash flow.

But if you don't feel comfortable with this concept, then the next best thing is a principal and interest loan over a long term – a minimum of 20 years. In the early stages, the principal and interest loan repayments will be almost the same as an interest-only payment and it will only be in the latter years of the loan, that any tax advantages will diminish.

Is the interest calculated in arrears or advance?

Interest paid monthly in advance is about 0.2% dearer than monthly in arrears. The difference is the interest on the interest for the fraction of the year that you have the use of the money, before the interest is due. For example, one month in arrears at 15% is $0.15 \times 0.15 \times (1/12)$, which is around 0.2% (i.e. 15% in advance is equivalent to 15.2% in arrears).

Can the interest be paid a full year in advance?

Paying the interest in advance can be an extremely useful strategy for reducing a tax liability that you suddenly become aware of near the end of a financial year. For instance, you can pay a whole year's interest in advance in May, and claim that expense in your June tax returns, regardless of how little rent you have earned. This has the effect of deferring tax for a full year. You could even receive a tax refund within one month of purchasing a property if you bought it in May, settled in June, and paid the interest one year in advance. To qualify as a legitimate tax deduction, you must receive some commercial advantage other than simply a tax saving. This is usually achieved by getting a reduced rate of interest on the loan in question. If you're considering paying the interest in advance, be wary of bank bills. Although the money, including the interest, is "loaned" in advance, the interest is paid when the loan becomes due and therefore cannot be claimed in advance.

Is interest calculated on daily or monthly balances?

With investment loans, unlike your first-home loan, there should be no need to make additional payments. However, if you have a principal and interest loan and you wish to pay extra, you should be aware that daily calculations are better than monthly. If you make a lump sum repayment at the beginning of the month on a loan where the interest is calculated monthly, you would effectively be giving the bank the loan of your money for a month, interest-free.

How often can the interest be paid?

If you have an interest-only loan, some lending institutions may be prepared to be flexible on the frequency of interest payments (i.e. monthly, quarterly or yearly). Consider the reverse situation; would you prefer to receive interest monthly (and get interest on your interest) or yearly. So too with borrowing money, and 14% interest paid quarterly in arrears is a lower effective rate than 14% paid yearly in advance. Most banks do not offer this option, and the standard monthly in arrears usually applies, but for those that do, the interest rate should be adjusted accordingly.

Can the interest be capitalised?

Some "low-start" loans are advertised with interest rates as low as 5% below the market rate. With these loans, initial repayments reflect the lower rate, but the remaining interest is capitalised (added to the principal). For example, on a loan of $150,000 with an interest rate of 15%, you would normally pay $22,500 interest for one year. If however, you take a low-start rate of 10% on a $150,000 loan, then in the first year you pay $15,000 in interest. The remaining 5% or $7,500 is added to the loan so that after one year you owe $157,500. Depending on whether you use a "cash" or "accrual" method of accounting, the capitalised interest may or may not be tax deductible. If this sounds confusing – it is. So if you are thinking of capitalising the interest, check with your accountant to see if it applies to your personal situation.

Borrowing Costs

As well as interest charges, there are costs of setting up loans and these are usually referred to as borrowing or loan costs. They are tax deductible against income (see chapter 15). These costs are the main trade-off when comparing interest rates, as some institutions have high upfront costs and low interest rates, whereas others have low upfront costs and higher interest rates. Borrowing costs can be divided into those charged by the financier and those charged by the government. The following questions will help you sort out the various borrowing costs.

How much are the establishment fees?

These may vary from nil to 4% or more of the loan. Sometimes, other costs are included in this initial upfront fee and it is important to know if this fee includes solicitor's fees, valuation fees etc, so that comparisons can be made with other lending institutions. A loan with an interest rate of 18% and no application or valuation fees might be suitable for a short-term (which you don't want). However, an interest rate of 14% fixed with a 1.5% application fee covering all upfront costs would be more attractive for the long-term investor (hopefully, that's you).

What is the cost of the application fees?

In most instances, the establishment fee and application fee is one and the same fee. However, some institutions may charge a non-refundable application fee of a few hundred dollars when you first apply for the loan, and a second fee called the establishment fee when you actually go ahead. Financial institutions are simply in the business of "selling" money as a commodity so, usually the "loan arranger" receives a commission for marketing the money. Now there's nothing sinister about this modus operandi except that you should be aware that this is the reason for these upfront costs in the first place.

How much are the valuation fees?

Some institutions charge nothing for valuations but the standard fee is approximately $1.50 per $1,000. This can vary depending on location, number of properties and whether or not it's a revaluation by the same financial institution.

How much are the mortgagee's solicitor's fees?

Solicitors acting for the lending institution (the mortgagee's solicitor) charge fees for preparation of the mortgage documentation. They may be "in house" or from an external firm of solicitors. Accordingly, these fees may vary from nil to about $1,000 on a $100,000 loan, with many solicitors charging a percentage of the scale rate. If the lending institution requires the services of an external solicitor, these fees will be unavoidable for although you can choose whether you use a solicitor for conveyancing, you won't be allowed to do the mortgage documentation yourself.

Is there mortgage insurance and what is the cost?

Some institutions charge you mortgage insurance premiums. They are paid once for each term of the loan. This insurance, taken out by the financial institution, is not to be confused with mortgage repayment insurance that protects you by covering your mortgage repayment if you are ill or lose your job etc. If you fail to meet the obligations of your loan, the mortgagee can sell your property, and claim from the mortgage insurers any shortfall between the loan and the selling price. It's not unusual for a financial institution to approve a loan "subject to approval by the mortgage insurers". It's also not unusual for one to approve, and the other to disapprove.

Mortgage insurance premiums vary depending on the loan/value ratio (L/V). Some banks may waive mortgage insurance altogether on all loans while others require it on loans only where the L/V ratio is more than 75%. Most institutions regard the 75% L/V ratio as their preferred lending option, but in poor economic times they might drop this to 65%. A guide to the rates of mortgage insurance is:

Loan/Value Ratio	Premium
65% to 75%	0.24% of loan (3 yrs)
65% to 75%	0.32% of loan (5 yrs)
76% to 80%	0.90% of loan (3 yrs)
76% to 80%	1.20% of loan (5 yrs)
81% to 85%	1.20% of loan (3 yrs)
81% to 85%	1.60% of loan (5 yrs)

Plus up to 5% of the premium for stamp duty

What are the penalty costs for early repayment?

With flexible loans, there may be no penalties for early repayment. In other cases, usually where the interest rate is fixed, the penalty may be as high as four months interest. I don't consider penalties a huge barrier, as they are part and parcel of less flexible lower-interest loans. But if you are unsure how to arrange your mortgages, don't lock into a very high penalty mortgage that will be costly to refinance later.

Can the mortgage be transferred and is there a cost?

In some cases, a mortgage may be transferred to another property, and if so, there may be a cost. This exchange is called substitution of collateral. If you have properties that have substantially increased in value, you may wish to re-arrange a mortgage, perhaps to unencumber a property for further mortgaging. For example, supposing you have a property worth $100,000, carrying a loan of $80,000. If this property increases in value over time to $200,000, it may be advantageous to shift the mortgage on to a less valuable property and in so doing, free up more equity. There may be revaluation costs, additional loan application fees and more solicitor's costs, but it may give you the flexibility to do other things with your unencumbered property.

How much are the administration charges?

There may be a small ($1 – $10) monthly fee that is fairly standard. The ones to watch out for are the yearly charges of $800 plus. These charges can effectively add another 1% to the interest rate.

How much is the brokerage fee?

A broker will charge you up to 1% to find you a source of finance. This may still work out cheaper and easier for you, but it pays to be wary. Some brokers have a direct inroad to the source of money and the 1% may also cover the application and brokerage fee. (Remember, money is a marketable commodity, and as such can be bought and sold by registered dealers who add a margin.) For those brokers who act purely as the go-between, the 1% may be in addition to a 1% application fee.

Is life insurance required and what is the cost?

Life insurance may be compulsory with some loans, in which case it would be tax deductible. It's a good idea to have it anyway, but be sure that you are not coerced into taking additional coverage with the lender if it is not really needed.

How much are the mortgage release fees?

Apart from the government's mortgage release fees, your financial institution may charge you additional release fees. These fees may be simply the cost of releasing the registered mortgage. Or if you are trying to release one property from a multi-property mortgage, it may include such costs as the mortgagee's solicitor's fees (~$300+), the mortgagee's re-arrangement fees (~$300+), increased mortgage insurance on existing properties (~$300+), and revaluation fees of other properties(~$300+).

How much are the rollover fees?

When you take out a fixed loan for a fixed period (e.g. fixed or variable interest-only loans over three years), rolling over with the same institution for a further period may cost money. This fee can be almost nothing, or quite substantial (more than $1,000), depending on whether there are solicitors involved. This is a real cost and should be taken into account in the first place when finding the best loan. It may also determine whether you rollover with the same lender, or seek alternative sources of finance. Rollover fees are not applicable to P & I loans.

Government charges associated with borrowing

Each state government levies a range of charges that vary between the states. They will be the same within each state, no matter who you use for finance. A reasonable guide to these charges is as follows:

- Stamp duty on mortgage: about 0.43% of the loan
- Registration of title: about $77 but varies with state
- Registration of mortgage: about $77 but varies with state
- Stamp duty on mortgage insurance: 5% of premium
- Stamp duty on mortgage release: about $1
- Mortgage release: about $77 but varies with state

A typical example of loan costs

If you bought a property for $100,000, with purchase costs of $2,700 and borrowing costs of $1,800, your total loan would be $104,500 if you borrowed the lot. A typical set of borrowing costs for a loan of $104,500 could be:

Loan Costs	
Establishment fee (.5% of loan)	522
Stamp duty on mortgage (0.43%)	450
Mortgage insurance	–
Mortgagee's solicitor's fees	636
Valuation fees	100
Registration of mortgage	77
Search fees	15
TOTAL	**$1,800**

13
Sources of
Finance

Where do you borrow money for your investment property? Good real estate agents can help you find the right property, but just as important is a good bank manager to help you finance it. You should spend more time looking for the right finance, than looking for the right property. It's not always best to "bank where you've always banked". However, when you find a good bank manager who understands all your needs, and is ready to assist you when others snub your goals, stick to him – or her. They can make borrowing money a painless, pleasant process and quite often, it's worth paying an additional 1% interest (.5% after-tax).

But be prepared for brick walls and don't be disillusioned by the first "no". I have known people on very high incomes to be turned down for a loan, just because the financier refused to take into account the tax savings resulting from the property investments. This happened to a person I know with an income of $100,000, and a tax bill of $40,000. Fortunately he persevered, and eventually found a very willing financier who is now the richer for this client's custom. Within six months of this happening, property prices increased by 30% and this person was laughing all the way to his new bank! How much will a "no" cost you?

The lending rules set by financial institutions are usually conservative to accommodate first-home buyers and first-time property investors. This can be stifling to your property investment program. The basic rule of most institutions is:

30% Salary + 80% Rent = Total Interest Payments

(Note: The total interest payments include existing mortgage payments, car payments and all other hire purchase costs.)

Now of course, this formula may suit the average person, but it does not suit all investors. It basically assumes that people spend one third of their income on living costs, one third on committed payments such as rent or interest and one third on tax. The flaw in the argument is two-fold. Firstly, it does not account for the substantial tax benefits, and secondly, it assumes that someone earning $200,000 a year has a grocery bill of one-third of their income – or $66,000! Rules may give you a guide-line, but do not necessarily give a true picture of the individual's situation. Before you apply for a loan, do your homework. Do your own cash flow and assets / liabilities statements to re-assure the financier that you are in control. There's no need to fabricate figures – it only risks a black mark against your name *when* you're found out. Ask for the amount you want and know you can handle – never ask "How much will you lend me?"

Generally speaking, the higher the interest rate, the more flexible the loan and, the lower the interest rate, the lower the flexibility (i.e. once you're in, you're in, and it's difficult to either sell the property or re-arrange the loan without incurring penalties). Below are some sources of finance.

Traditional Banks
e.g. ANZ, National, Commonwealth, Westpac

In the past, the big four banks were not a good source of finance to investors of residential property. Traditionally, they favoured big business through the trading divisions, and first-home buyers through the savings divisions. However, with the recent spate of corporate collapses and the resultant "bad debts", a few of these banks have at long last recognised the security in lending to residential property investors and have become fairly competitive. Although they tend to have lower upfront costs, interest rates are usually higher but they can be negotiable on this.

Smaller Banks
e.g. Metway, Advance Bank, Bank of Melbourne

These banks have evolved from the building societies and are a first rate source of finance because of their traditional origins with property finance. My experience has been that they seem to have down-to-earth philosophies and approachable managers. The borrowing costs and interest rates are quite reasonable, and they offer a good middle-of-the-road type loan. Their biggest plus is that they will lend money on fairly high L/V ratios (up to 90%), and can usually offer second mortgages at the same rate as a first.

Building Societies and Credit Unions
e.g. Suncorp, St George

These are excellent for both first-home buyers and property investors. Their rates of interest are competitive and they have acceptable upfront charges. But they have strict rules applying to income levels and are not usually flexible if you don't fit the guidelines – even though you can well afford the loan. It's up to you to present your special case.

Trustee Companies
e.g. ANZ Trustees, Perpetual Trustees, Permanent Custodians, Permanent Trustees

These companies are difficult to find and much of their business is by word of mouth or through advertisements in the financial papers. Their interest rates can be about 2% below the market rate and this makes them very attractive for long-term property investors. But scaled against this are other factors that you have to weigh up. The upfront costs can be high, with mortgagee's solicitor's fees as well as high establishment costs. The mortgages are usually inflexible, and there may be high penalty costs. As well as this, whenever you rollover the loan at the end of the term (usually three or five years), there are more establishment costs and solicitor's fees. Also, these types of financial institutions usually require a good deal of collateral, and consequently they can tie up a large amount of property for a small loan. However, despite these drawbacks, I believe these are a great source of finance for seasoned long-term property investors.

Finance Companies
e.g. Esanda, Beneficial Finance

In general, finance companies have almost non-existent upfront fees, but high interest rates. There are a few small finance companies that are exceptions and these tend to be more like the trustee companies. Finance companies are more suited to developers and traders in property, where short-term commitments might lessen the impact of higher interest rates. But as a rule, they aren't suitable for long-term property investors.

Private Finance
e.g. Solicitors' Trust Accounts

Before the deregulation of the financial markets made access to money much easier, it was standard practice to borrow funds from accountants' and solicitors' clients. This method is still used to a limited degree. Family members may also be a good source of finance and sometimes it may not be necessary to pay any upfront fees at all, nor even register the mortgage. However, tread very warily when dealing with finance within the family. Misunderstandings and disputes over money can cause disharmony and may not be worth it.

Vendor Finance
Vendor finance is almost non-existent in Australia. In a few cases, the vendor will carry back a first or second mortgage – but be wary – a lower interest rate is usually coupled with a higher purchase price. In Australia, less than 1% of loans are vendor financed whereas in America, almost 90% of sales involve either vendor finance or assumable mortgages (i.e. the mortgage is tied to the property, not the person). As a result, most of the

American books on the subject of property investment are about creatively manipulating the finance, not the price! And then it really doesn't matter what the property price is, so long as the interest payments are low. So if you read these excellent books (see chapter 20), remember that it doesn't quite work the same way here in Australia. I often see advertisements placed by hopeful investors trying to emulate the American techniques. One such advertisement read:

FULL PRICE. I am willing to pay full price for your property if you are willing to sell on flexible terms (little or no money down). Call Jim: 00005 1234 – 1050.

This works fine in the United States – but not here in Australia.

Overseas Finance

Loans with very low interest rates are available if you borrow from overseas, but they are extremely risky because of the fluctuating dollar. If the principal of your loan is in a foreign currency, the debt can rise dramatically if the $A falls. You could see yourself going backwards and finish up owing more than what you borrowed. So unless you are prepared to hedge against a drop in the dollar, stay well clear. Many an investor has been caught in this trap, and while it appears very attractive on the way in, it can be very costly on the way out.

Insurance Companies
e.g. GIO, National Mutual

It is possible to borrow money through insurance companies or other fund management companies, as some of their funds are invested in first mortgages. They can be an excellent source of finance, similar to that offered by the trustee companies – low interest rates, but low L/V ratios and usually high penalties. It's also possible to borrow against the value of any life assurance policies you may have with such a company. Some insurance companies will lend you up to 90% of the amount you have placed with them and usually at competitive interest rates.

International Banks
e.g. Citibank, Chase AMP

These banks usually offer innovative investment loans that are quite attractive, probably because they may be more experienced in "marketing money" than their Australian counterparts. They can be a good source of finance, particularly if they are innovative enough to appreciate your needs as a property investor.

14
Costs of Buying and Selling

The costs associated with buying and selling property (capital costs) should not be confused with the borrowing costs that are associated with finance. The taxation implications for buying and selling costs are totally different to borrowing costs. Borrowing costs are directly tax deductible by spreading the costs over several years (see chapter 15). However, buying and selling costs are not tax deductible directly against income and are only accounted for in the capital gains tax calculations on sale.

Buying costs include your solicitor's fees for supervising the transfer of the property title (conveyancing) as well as the stamp duty on the contract. These solicitor's fees are separate to those of the financier's solicitor who prepares the mortgage documentation. The selling costs include your solicitor's fees for the conveyancing, the real estate agent's commission and any other costs related to the selling of the property.

The capital gains tax, which is indirectly a selling cost, is discussed in this chapter because it is incurred only on the sale of the property. As you will see, this tax has a minimal effect on long-term property investors. Unlike normal taxation records where the requirement for retention is only a few years, records of costs relating to the capital gains tax must be kept until the property is sold – which can be for twenty years or more. For this reason, you must keep strict records of *all* costs relating to property.

Buying Costs

Buying or purchasing costs are incurred whether the property is bought with borrowed money or not. You can borrow these costs as part of your loan and the interest will be tax deductible, but the actual purchase costs are not tax deductible. They will be inflation-indexed and accounted for in the capital gains tax on the sale of the property.

Stamp duty on purchase

This can be paid after settlement but within 30 days of signing the contract or your financier may insist that the stamp duty be paid before settlement. The rates vary from state to state and with the cost of the property, but in general, for a property priced between $100,000 and $160,000, the stamp duty will be between 2% and 3.5%. (Rates for owner-occupied property are usually lower than for investment property). Below is a sample of what you can expect to pay in stamp duty costs.

Typical Stamp Duties on Property (1992)

State	$100,000	$130,000	$160,000
Queensland	2,350	3,325	4,300
New South Wales	1,990	3,040	4,000
Victoria	2,200	4,000	5,800
South Australia	2,830	4,030	5,230
Western Australia	1,900	2,875	3,850
Northern Territory	2,100	3,000	3,950
Tasmania	2,425	3,325	4,275
ACT	2,015	3,065	4,225

Your solicitor's fees

Each state has its own scale of solicitors fees for conveyancing but generally, this is around $1,500 for a $100,000 property. In some states there are special "land brokers" who can do this conveyancing – usually at a cost well below that of solicitors. It is also possible to do the conveyancing and the searches yourself, but it is time consuming, mainly because of the number of forms involved. If you are trying this for the first time, use a "Do It Yourself" type legal service that will cost you about $90 – $180. If you have any doubts at all, use a solicitor.

Part of the solicitor's work is to conduct searches to ensure that your property is free of "liabilities" such as an impending main road. Search fees are charged by the various government departments to provide you with necessary information and documentation. These fees may vary, but as a guide to the costs, you should expect to pay approximately $100 to $200 for all the searches if handled by a solicitor.

If it was necessary for your solicitor to scrutinise the mortgage documents and conduct searches at the request of your financier, then a portion of your solicitor's fees may be classified as a borrowing cost for tax purposes.

Selling Costs

Before you contemplate selling, you should look at all the hidden costs that drain away your profits. Depending on the time it takes to sell a property (usually about three months), there may be an opportunity cost factor of lost rent; if tenants move out well in advance, this cost may be as high as $1800 ($150/week x 12 weeks). If you sell a property within a relatively short time of buying, and do it often enough, then you will be classed as a trader. In this instance, the capital gain will be classed as income and taxed at the full marginal rate of tax with no inflationary or averaging allowance (see next page for details on the Capital Gains Tax). If you bought a property for $85,000 and sold it within a year for $110,000, the real costs might look like this:

Costs of Selling

Agent's costs	$3,000
Solicitor's costs	$1,000
Renovation costs	$5,000
Mortgage release etc	$1,000
Interest	$10,000
Tax on profits	$2,000
(if classed as trader)	
TOTAL COSTS	**$22,000**

The total costs associated with selling could even be much higher than the $22,000 in this example. Where is the profit? I don't call a $3,000 return on an $85,000 investment a great return, especially if you've spent every weekend working on it! You don't want to pay this cost every few years, so stick to the plan – buy and keep and build-in your profits long term.

Your solicitor's fees

There is less work involved in selling than buying, so solicitor's fees on selling are consequently less. The fees may vary between states and depending on the type of property, but they should be negotiable. If you do it yourself, it's much easier to handle the conveyancing when you sell than when you buy.

Sales commission

This varies from state to state and is set on a sliding scale. As a rough guide for properties around $100,000, the commission works out to be approximately 3%. This should be taken into account when calculating any capital gains tax liability or profits on selling.

Capital Gains Tax

The Capital Gains Tax (CGT), introduced on September 19, 1985, has been seen by many investors as a discouragement to property investment. This shows a great misunderstanding of the tax as it was not designed to discourage investors but discourage short-term profit taking – and this it has done very effectively. If you follow the philosophy of investing long-term, and always "buy to keep", then you'll probably pay minimal CGT. If you do sell in the long-term, the effect of the tax is cushioned, as it is paid only on the gains over and above inflation. Even then, there are special averaging provisions so that, if your other sources of income are low (e.g. if you're retired or have other negatively geared property), you may pay little or no CGT at all. (These benefits are not afforded to investors with bank deposits, where interest is taxed without indexation).

According to the Taxation Office in its booklet entitled *"Income Tax and Capital Gains"*, the Indexed Cost Base is the cost base of a property after adjustment for inflation. The cost base includes acquisition costs (purchase price and purchase costs), improvement costs (if any), disposal costs, and any incidental capital costs, all of which can be indexed for inflation. For example, the purchase price would be indexed thus:

$$\text{Indexed Purchase Price} = \frac{\text{Index on sale}}{\text{Index on purchase}} \times \text{Purchase Price}$$

The CPI Indices (available from the Taxation Office) are listed below.

CPI Indices

Qtr	End	Index	Qtr	End	Index	Qtr	End	Index	Qtr	End	Index
1985	Sep	144.2	1987	Mar	164.7	1988	Sep	182.4	1990	Mar	204.1
	Dec	147.1		Jun	167.2		Dec	186.4		Jun	207.4
1986	Mar	150.5		Sep	170.0	1989	Mar	188.0		Sep	208.9
	Jun	153.0		Dec	172.0		Jun	192.6		Dec	214.5
	Sep	157.0	1988	Mar	176.0		Sep	197.0	1991	Mar	214.1
	Dec	161.5		Jun	179.0		Dec	200.7		Jun	214.4

Note: The index number on sale is based on the contract date, not the settlement date.

There are two separate steps in calculating the CGT on the sale of a property. Firstly, the capital gain is calculated from the Indexed Cost Base and this is the same result regardless of a person's income. Secondly, the capital gains tax is then worked out and this result depends entirely on the income of the investor. Let's consider an example to see how this works.

A house bought in February 1988 for $50,000 was sold in March 1998 (10 years later) for $130,000. Purchase costs (stamp duty and solicitor's fees) were $2,000 and disposal costs (sales commission and solicitor's fees) were $5,500. Improvements worth $2,010 were done in July 1989. The index number at purchase was 176, at the time of improvements was 197 and on sale was 380 (estimated at 8% inflation). The real capital gain is:

$130,000 – ($50,000 + $2,000 + $2,010 + $5,500) = $70,490

However, the taxable capital gain is just $8,349 (see below).

Step 1.   Calculating the Taxable Capital Gain

Sale price	= $130,000	
Indexed acquisition costs	= $112,273	(380/176) x (50,000 + 2,000)
Indexed improvement costs	= $3,878	(380/197) x 2,010
Disposal costs	= $5,500	
Indexed Cost Base	= $121,651	
Taxable capital gain	= $8,349	(130,000 – 121,651)

Step 2.   Calculating the Capital Gains Tax

		$0	$30,000	$50,000
1	Taxable Income	$0	$30,000	$50,000
2	Tax on Income	0	$6,594	$15,314
3	Capital Gain	$8,349	$8,349	$8,349
4	1/5 the Capital Gain (Line 3 divided by 5)	$1,670	$1,670	$1,670
5	1/5th Gain + Income (Line 1 + Line 4)	$1,670	$31,670	$51,670
6	New Tax on (1/5th Gain + Income)	$0	$7,228	$16,099
7	Additional Tax (Line 6 – Line 2)	$0	$634	$785
8	**Capital Gains Tax** (Line 7 multiplied by 5)	**$0**	**$3,170**	**$3,925**

Note: Taxes exclude Medicare Levy, which is paid on the full capital gain.

These three examples show you how both indexation and averaging can reduce the CGT to a negligible amount compared to the real gain of $70,490. Even for someone earning $50,000, CGT is only $3,925. For a person with no taxable income, there would be no CGT at all because of the averaging effects. This situation might also apply if the property was in the name of the highest-income earner, but sold in a year when he had many other negatively geared properties or, alternatively, when he retired.

15
Typical Tax Deductions

Recently, a person at a seminar admitted to me that he owned a rental property which he let for $100 per week and that for the last three years, he had not declared the rent in his tax return for fear of paying tax on his little retirement nest egg. He had a small loan of $30,000 on the property with interest at $4,200 per year. With rates and insurances at $800, he figured he was up for tax of $80 on the profit of $200 per year ($5,200 rent less $5,000 costs, at around 40% marginal tax rate).

However, when *all* of the tax deductions were considered, we discovered that he was owed a large tax refund. He had neglected to take into account the deductions for borrowing costs, depreciation, and travel. These travel deductions were substantial as he collected the rent each week via a 50 kilometre round trip in his four wheel drive. All in all, he was entitled to a tax refund of $700 this year alone. His fear and lack of understanding of the tax laws had probably cost him a few thousand dollars over the years!

So make sure you claim your full entitlements. However, the new substantiation rules put the onus on you to be able to support your claims by documentation – don't take the risk of unsupported claims. It's best to check with your accountant to satisfy yourself that your investments are structured tax effectively. Accountants may not be experts in showing you how to build wealth through investment property, but they should be able to expertly answer your questions and prepare your tax returns. But don't simply give him a shoe-box full of receipts and expect him to do the rest.

However, tax deductions must be put in perspective because no matter how many pencils, rubbers, rulers and stamps you claim, they are trivial compared to the largest tax deduction of all – interest on your borrowings. Without interest, your tax deductions will pale into insignificance.

Tax deductions for rental property fall into two categories – capital costs and revenue costs.

Capital Costs

Capital costs include buying and selling costs, and improvement costs. The buying and selling costs have been discussed in chapter 14, so now let's take a close look at what constitutes an improvement. There is a thin grey line between what you would like to call a repair (to make it tax deductible now) and an improvement (which is tax deductible in relation to the capital gains tax on sale). Repairs are defined as the maintenance that restores the property to its original condition when you bought it – not the original value when it was built. Improvements make the property better than when you bought it.

One of the most often asked questions is, "If I buy a rental property, how long do I have to wait before I can claim the painting as a repair?" Although various well-meaning people provide answers ranging from one to three years, the truth of the matter is that the taxation office sets no fixed time limit for claiming such repairs. For example, if you bought a rental property that needed painting immediately and you held off for one year to paint it, the taxation office could well disallow your claim on the grounds that the property needed painting at the time of purchase. However, if you bought a property in immaculate condition and after one day, the tenant dismantled a motorcycle in the living room (highly unlikely) necessitating repainting immediately, then the cost of repainting should be tax deductible. This is a case of restoring the property to the condition in which it was bought, even though the repairs were carried out shortly after purchase.

If you buy a property that needs painting immediately, don't hold off for a few years in the hope that the painting costs will be tax deductible at a later date. It is far better to paint at once, even though it is not tax deductible – not only does it improve the value of the property, but it makes the property easier to let and probably at a higher rent.

There is also a subtlety in doing "repairs". For example, if you re-roof an old rusted iron-roofed house with iron, it would probably be considered a repair. But if you were to use tiles, it would probably be classed as an improvement.

Although you cannot claim the cost of improvements immediately, you can borrow the money for them and claim the interest. Also, if you have made substantial improvements to your property since September 16, 1987, they should qualify for the capital allowance of 2.5%. This means that at least some of the improvement costs are tax deductible. If, for example, you built a carport for your rental property and the total costs were $4,800, you would be able to claim $120 each year for 40 years.

Revenue Costs

Revenue costs are directly deductible against rental income. These deductions may be either cash and non-cash. Cash deductions such as rates and interest cost you real cash from your pocket. But non-cash deductions such as depreciation and borrowing costs are claimed in your tax return, without costing you cash. A list of typical deductions is set out below showing both cash and non-cash deductions. These claims are based on a property purchased for $100,000 with a loan of $104,500 ($4,500 costs) at a fixed interest rate of 14%. Rent is $160 per week ($8,320 per year).

Typical Taxation Deductions

	Deductions	Cash	Non-Cash
Rates	900	900	
Fire Levy	70	70	
Insurance	100	100	
Interest on Borrowings	14,630	14,630	
Borrowing Costs	600		600
Agent's Commission	724		724 *
Letting Fee	160	160	
Accounting Fee	160		160 *
Repairs	100	100	
Cleaning / Pest Control	84	84	
Gardening	116		116 *
Depreciation	2,700		2,700
Advertising	20	20	
Telephone	20	20	
Stationery / Postage	20	20	
Travelling Allowance	190	190	
Total Deductions	**$20,594**	**$16,294**	**$4,300**

* Either cash or non-cash deductions depending on circumstances.

It can be very deceiving to calculate the deductions solely on the basis of real cash costs. In the above example, these would come to $16,294, yet non-cash costs add $4,300 to the claims. Most of these non-cash costs are depreciation and borrowing costs, but some (as in the example above) may be payments to family who have been responsible for such things as property management, accounting or gardening, in which case these costs would appear as income on the family member's taxation returns. But if his/her income is less than $5,400, this would incur no additional tax.

Check List of Tax Deductions

Below is a check list for many of the deductions you can claim against your income-producing investment property. Perhaps you can think of more that might relate to your own individual situation.

Local government charges

These include all local government charges, such as general rates, water rates, garbage collection, sewerage and, if applicable, registration fees for flats etc. If you have just bought a rental property, the portion paid on settlement is tax deductible.

Fire levy

This varies and could be collected by local governments, or could be a separate account levied by the state government.

Insurance

Both property and contents insurance are tax deductible. It may also be possible to claim your personal life insurance, but only if your financier insisted on it as part of the loan conditions.

Interest on borrowings

Money can be borrowed for the following: Purchase costs, borrowing costs, repairs, improvements, interest in advance, cash flow deficit throughout the first year, and maintenance etc. If the loan is fixed-interest, interest-only, the amount will be constant each year. If the loan is principal and interest, just the interest component of the repayment is tax deductible and, because the principal is being paid off, the annual interest deduction will decline. If you are building an investment property for rental purposes, the interest repayments are deductible during construction time. Likewise, if you have a property that you are trying to rent but can't, or if a property is vacant for several months while you are renovating, the interest is deductible over the vacant period, providing you can demonstrate a future intent to rent.

Borrowing costs

These can be deducted over five years or the term of the loan, which ever is the lesser period. They include all costs associated with the loan (application fees, valuation fees, mortgagee's solicitor's fees, mortgage insurance, search fees required by mortgagee, registration of mortgage, stamp duty on mortgage, broker's fees, etc – see chapter 12 for detail). If you sell your property, still with borrowing costs yet to be claimed, the remainder may be claimed in that year. Also, if the property is sold or refinanced, the fees for releasing the mortgage (registration plus bank handling fees) are deductible in that particular year.

Agent's commission

Agent's fees for both letting and managing the rental property are tax deductible and can amount to between 5% and 30% of gross rent depending on the agent and if the property is for holiday letting. Although it is much better to use a professional property manager, your spouse could possibly act as your agent and this can be very tax effective if he/she is not working. You could even pay an agent a letting fee to find the tenant and then you or your spouse take over the management.

Accounting fees

Although, it is wise to use a professional accountant to prepare your tax returns, if your spouse has been involved in some of the accounting and banking procedures for your properties, then he/she can be paid according to the number of hours worked. But again, it will only become tax effective if his/her marginal tax rate is lower than yours.

Repairs

These include painting, fence repairs, re-tiling, roof-fixing – in fact, just about anything that can be classed as property maintenance, but check the distinction between repairs and improvements as outlined earlier. It is very tax-effective to have repairs carried out toward the end of the financial year (in say May or June). If you do the repairs yourself, you can't claim for your time, unless of course the property is in the name of your spouse. If the property is jointly owned, you can charge your spouse half of the costs of repair, but the fee must also be added to your income – in which case it may not be worth your while to do so.

Cleaning/Pest control

This includes carpet cleaning, internal and external wall cleaning as well as stoves etc. Pest control will also help keep the property clean. Depending on the terms of the lease, these costs may be at the tenant's expense and can be redeemed from the bond if the tenant has not already paid for them. It is possible to employ your spouse or your children (if they are capable) to carry out these duties between tenancies.

Gardening

The costs of having the lawns mowed and trees trimmed are tax deductible. Generally, tenants should be responsible for mowing and keeping the yard tidy but again, you can give your family members the opportunity to earn some pocket money. The hiring of trailers or any other equipment needed is also tax deductible. When you buy mower fuel, pay for it separately at the garage and get a receipt. But be careful not to undertake major landscaping projects and expect to claim the costs. Unless it is normal maintenance, it could well be classed as an improvement.

Depreciation of fittings and furniture

Depreciation is the method of writing off the wear and tear on assets used to produce income. These claims do not apply to shares and give property another special advantage. When you first purchase a property, it is your responsibility to set fair market value on the depreciable items as they exist in the property at the time (not what they cost when new). The "value" of the item includes the cost, installation cost, transportation cost, and a percentage of professional fees (architects etc) associated with the building.

The recent Economic Statement of February 26th, 1992 has introduced changes to the depreciation rules. Under the new arrangements, a seven band schedule will apply to property acquired, or where construction commenced, after February 26th, 1992 and depreciation is permissable only on the diminishing value method. (The diminishing value method has the advantage that it confers tax benefits earlier than the prime cost method.) However, just to confuse the issue further, if you have acquired several properties over the last decade, many different depreciating methods and rates may apply.

Outlined below is a list of the more common items and their current depreciation rates.

Depreciation Rates for Common Items

Item	DV(%)
Curtains	30
Carpets	25
Fluorescent lights	20
Hot water system	20
Lino (floor coverings)	25
TV sets	25
Refrigerator	20
Vacuum cleaner	25
Kitchen cupboards (removable)	20
Heating units	25
Washing machines	30
Microwave Ovens	30
Stoves	20

Note: Bedding, crockery, cutlery, linen, glassware, and cooking utensils are claimed as replacement value – not depreciated.

The example below shows how carpet (with an estimated value of $1,000 and depreciation rate of 25%) is depreciated using the diminishing value method. You can see that the amount claimed is higher in the first year, and is then reduced in the following years when the depreciation is calculated on the declining balance. In this case, the implied write-off life would be six years, at which time the depreciation benefits would cut out.

Depreciation Calculation

Year	Opening Written Down Value	Rate %	Depreciation Amount	Closing Written Down Value
1	$1,000	25	$250	$750
2	$750	25	$187.5	$562.5
3	$562.5	25	$140.5	$422

Where you have items that you use both privately as well as for your rental properties, you can still claim for a percentage of the depreciation. This can be done on a separate depreciation schedule. In this case, simply reduce the amount of the deduction by a fraction equivalent to that of private usage. Such items might include mower, power tools, sewing machine (for curtains), answering machine, computer, wheelbarrow, ladder etc. As a guide, if you have one rental property, the split might be 10% rental property and 90% private. By the time you have 15 properties, the split would more likely be 90% rental property and 10% private.

"Depreciation" of building (capital allowance)

Technically, this is not a depreciation claim but a capital allowance. It is not based on the cost of the building to the investor, but on the original construction cost. All residential property built for investment between July 17, 1985 and September 16, 1987, qualifies for a capital allowance of 4%. If it was constructed after September 16, 1987, then the allowance is 2.5%. Any improvements (e.g. garages, car ports, extensions, etc) built after that date also qualify for the 2.5% allowance. Below is an example of how this capital allowance works:

Capital Allowance Calculation

Property cost (building + land)	= $120,000
Land value	= $50,000 (irrelevant)
Current building value	= $70,000 (irrelevant)
Construction cost (estimate)	= $35,000 (relevant)
Capital allowance	= 2.5% of $35,000
	= $875 each yr for 40 yrs

In the calculation of the capital gains tax, the amount claimed for the building allowance is not "written back" on to the capital gain because it is not a part of the Indexed Cost Base. Many investors have been worried by the possibility that claiming the building allowance will increase the amount of capital gains tax, but this is not so. This confusion arises because the allowance is taken into account when calculating the reduced cost base (i.e. if you sell at a loss) but not when calculating the indexed cost base (i.e. when you sell at a profit).

Advertising

This may include newspaper advertisements to obtain tenants or tradesmen. If you advertise and need to buy newspapers regularly to check on market rent levels or even property prices, you may be able to claim a percentage of newspaper costs as well.

Telephone

The tenant is responsible for all costs associated with a telephone at the property. However, if there is no phone connection, and your tenant wants one, you should negotiate to pay a portion of the connection costs – if not all. There is a danger that if one tenant does not want a phone and allows the connection time to lapse, you could be up for a new connection fee when a new tenant moves in. As a precaution, you should ensure that there is a clause in the lease that compels the tenant to maintain the phone rental service even if he does not use it. Regarding the telephone used from your home, keep an accurate and detailed record of all calls for a set period (e.g. three months) and work out the percentage relating to property management compared to private use. You can use this ratio for future claims until the situation changes.

Stationery/Postage

All writing and office materials can be deducted in proportion to their business/private use. The first item you should buy is a spike or container to hold all those receipts until you get time to file them. As well as the stationery costs, you can claim the postage. It's amazing how often you pay rental property bills, bank charges and other costs by mail. When you go to the post office for a set of stamps used solely for management of your rental properties, ask for a dated docket.

Travelling allowance

If you collect the rent, do the repairs or simply drive past to check the property, you should be able to claim a car allowance. Make a regular habit of driving past each of your investment properties and if it looks good from the outside, it will probably be good on the inside. If you have many properties and exceed 5,000 km per year, there are methods other than the "per km" for claiming car expenses. The following are the per km rates for the 91/92 financial year:

Normal engine	Car Allowance Rotary engine	Rate / km
Up to 1600 cc	Up to 800 cc	41.1c
1601 to 2000 cc	801 to 1000 cc	49.9c
2001 to 3000 cc	1001 to 1500 cc	52.4c
Over 3000 cc	Over 1500 cc	55.9c

Do a three month trial logbook and work out the percentage of travel attributable on a yearly basis to your rental property. This percentage may then be used for all future claims until the situation changes. If you need to travel interstate for any reason relating to the management of your properties, you can claim your return airfare, accommodation and meal costs accordingly.

Bank charges

Most of the bank charges will be taken care of in your loan costs. However, if you use a bankcard or cheque book for payment of property expenses, you may claim a percentage of your cheque account / bankcard charges according to the amount of rental property use.

Electricity/Heating/Cooling

Usually, this is the tenant's responsibility, but if not, you should claim it. You can also claim the costs of any re-connection fee, if this is applicable. If heating is by some method other than electricity, such as wood or coal for a fireplace, then this can be claimed separately.

Legal expenses

These include expenses for lease preparation, tenant eviction, etc. The lease is usually prepared by the managing agent and hopefully, any dispute that arises over the lease agreement can be sorted out long before legal action is necessary.

Body corporate fees

These pertain to unit owners and will vary depending on the rent and unit value. Although the fees can be several hundred dollars, they may include building insurance, cleaning and external repairs to the complex. It's usual for some of the money collected in fees to be channelled into a "sinking fund" for any major repairs at some time in the future.

Land tax

Land tax varies from state to state but you can usually jointly own a few properties between a husband and wife before you exceed the tax-free limits. The family home is usually omitted from the calculations.

Recent changes in some states, together with rapid increases in land valuations have meant that some land tax charges have risen sharply over the last few years. The tax deductibility of these costs lessens the impact and, in the longer term, has only a small effect on future returns.

Worker's compensation

Insurance for worker's compensation will vary from state to state and is usually only a small cost, but well worthwhile. It covers you in the event that the handyman who has neglected to take out worker's compensation insurance may fall off the roof of your rental property and hurt himself. He could then make a claim back on you.

Business deductions

When you own many rental properties, you are effectively operating a business, and there may be a separate list of deductions that relate to this. These claims may form part of your property deductions, or may constitute a separate section under the general heading of business deductions.

Such a list might include – property investment manuals; investment magazines; newspapers; seminars; books; car claims and depreciation on equipment (e.g. desk, chair, bookshelves, computer, wheelbarrow, books, filing cabinet). This list may also include any of the costs already listed as property deductions, but which are difficult to apportion to each property (e.g. mower fuel – how much did you use where?).

There would also be costs associated with a home-office or "place of business" but there is a subtle difference between the two. Home-office costs might include telephone, lighting and depreciation, but if it is called your "place of business" (a particular place set aside for business only), then additional claims for rates, insurances, repairs and interest may be made. Claims are based on the percentage of the floor area used as an office. However, if your home was purchased after September 19, 1985, and you claim your costs as a "place of business", you may jeopardise your home's status as being free of capital gains tax.

16
Negative Gearing

We have all heard the term "negative gearing" bandied around, but what exactly does it mean? Let me explain the term. When referring to real estate, gearing (or leverage) is when you use some of your own money together with some other people's money (OPM) to control a large amount of property. The only way you can use OPM, is to borrow it and when you borrow a large amount of money, such that the interest payments exceed the rent, the result is a negative cash flow or "loss". The property is then said to be negatively geared.

Current legislation enables you to offset this "loss" against your income from any other source. This is providing that the property is income-producing and that you intend to earn a positive income from the property eventually. (Which of course you do). Your "other income" might be from your salaried job, business, other properties or bank cash deposits. The "loss" from your rental properties usually results in a tax refund which lessens the impact of the "loss".

But the purpose of these "losses" is not simply to get a healthy tax refund. So why continue to make such "losses" on rental properties? Why pay out all this money year after year? When do you stop making losses and start making money? I liken it to growing an apple tree. You plant the seeds, water and nurture them until they sprout, then fertilize them for many years until one day the tree bears apples for you to pick. And year after year your apple tree continues to grow and produce apples that you can pick and enjoy whenever you want.

Borrowing, buying and keeping rental properties works the same way. In the short-term, you feed your properties money – *you* have to make up the difference between the interest bill and what the tenant and taxman contribute. Over many years, while you are still working, you continue to direct money into your rental properties. But in the long-term, you reap the rewards with the capital gain and the increased rent providing you with a wealthy retirement. How many seeds of wealth are you going to plant and how often are you going to feed and water them?

Tax Benefits

The current tax scales (see below) are such that the harder you work, the more you earn, the more tax you pay. Well the great thing about borrowing to buy rental property is that the harder you work, the more you earn, the more tax you get back. But negative gearing is not just for the high-income earners. I believe that anyone who wants to build wealth by investing in rental property will benefit no matter what their income level.

1991/1992 Tax Scales

Income	Marginal Rate
Below $5,400	nil
$5,400 to $20,700	20%
$20,700 to $36,000	38%
$36,000 to $50,000	46%
Over $50,000	47%

Note: Medicare Levy (1.25%) to be added to incomes over $11,745

If you earn more than $50,000, you will be paying tax on your "top" dollars at 48.25% (47% + 1.25% medicare levy). Consequently, the tax deductions that you can make will be "saving" tax at the same rate i.e. 48.25%. Let's see how borrowing to buy an investment property affects different incomes. Assume an investment property costs $100,000 and is bought with a loan of $104,500 ($4,500 for costs). Rent is $160/week ($8,320/year), and total deductions are $20,594 for the first year.

Tax Savings on a $100,000 Rental Property

Current Income	$20,000	$30,000	$40,000	$50,000
Current Tax	$3,170	$6,969	$11,214	$15,939
Rent	$8,320	$8,320	$8,320	$8,320
Deductions	$20,594	$20,594	$20,594	$20,594
Loss	$12,274	$12,274	$12,274	$12,274
New Taxable Income	$7,726	$17,726	$27,726	$37,726
New Tax	$465	$2,687	$6,076	$10,140
TAX REFUND	$2,705	$4,282	$5,138	$5,799

Note: Taxes include Medicare

From the examples, you can see that "negative gearing" applied to property investments favours the higher-income earner. For someone earning $20,000, the tax savings would be $2,705, while for an income of $50,000, the same property, with the same loan and same tenants would produce a tax refund of $5,799. This is certainly not an indication that lower-income earners should not invest in property, but simply, the tax benefits are not as great. But what it does indicate is that negatively geared property should be bought in the name of the highest-income earner.

One thing to note in these calculations is that the resulting taxable income is not "all" that you have left to live on. As I said earlier, there are non-cash deductions such as depreciation and borrowing costs that could increase an apparently low taxable income by $3,000 to $4,000 or more. So when you have a few investment properties, your taxable income may approach zero, but your cash flow could be thousands of dollars because of the non-cash deductions. For example, if you had seven properties, all with non-cash deductions of about $3,000 – your cash flow would be $21,000 per year, even though your taxable income may be zero!!

One of the questions investors could well ask is, "But will negative gearing continue? The Government has stopped it once, could they do it again?" In 1985, the Government legislated to abolish the process of offsetting losses against other income. They didn't abolish the right to negatively gear, just the right to claim losses against other income. All losses were quarantined and could be offset against future rental gains. But this was relatively unattractive and property investors left the scene in a tidal wave, leaving in their wake such an extreme shortage of rental accommodation that the government was forced to repeal the legislation – just two years later in 1987. I doubt that they will change direction again but given this remote possibility, there are several points to consider.

First, no government can afford to house all the needy, so they are not likely to discourage investors by restricting the deductibility of losses. I suspect that it is probably more cost effective for investors to house the poor than it is for the government. Secondly, when they last restricted deductibility, it was not made retrospective so that investors who already had negatively geared rental property could still claim the losses against other income. And thirdly, if restrictions were re-introduced, you would still be able to gear property by borrowing, but it would then be a matter of matching the interest payments to the rent so that there is no shortfall.

Yet another important point is the fact that if the laws are tampered with, many investors will shy away from the property market. This could again lead to an imbalance in the supply and demand for rental properties and result in a meteoric rise in rents. This aspect has been recognised by Dr Ron Silberberg (National Director of Housing Industry Australia) who was reported in the Courier Mail (September 23rd, 1991) as saying that rents would skyrocket if negative gearing on rental housing was not retained. This was exactly the experience of the 1985 to 1987 fiasco.

Section 221D

One of the most limiting factors in buying rental property, particularly if you are a PAYE taxpayer, is meeting the cash flow deficit in the first 12 months. Normally, you have to wait for between 12 and 24 months for your tax refund. However, if you are a PAYE taxpayer, you can alleviate this burden by applying for a reduction in your PAYE tax. Section 221D of the Taxation Act allows for PAYE taxpayers with large predictable tax reductions, to reduce their fortnightly or monthly instalments, rather than wait to get a tax refund. (If you are paying provisional tax, you can have your provisional payments altered.) To obtain a variation, you will need to fill out the special form, "Application For Variation of Tax Instalment Deductions" provided by the Tax Office or write a letter along these lines:

Application for Tax Instalment Variation

> *J. Citizen*
> *123 Paye St.,*
> *Cleveland, 4163*
> *6th May, 1992*
>
> *The Variations Clerk*
> *Instalments Section*   *Tax File No 789 123 456*
> *City Taxation Office*   *Last lodged: Brisbane, 1989*
> *GPO Box 9900*
> *City X001*
> *Dear Sir,*
>
>   *As I have recently purchased a rental property, my financial situation has changed and I wish to apply under Section 221D of the Taxation Act to have my fortnightly PAYE instalments revised accordingly. Below are details of my projected tax liabilities for this financial year. I trust that a reduction in my current PAYE tax instalments would be in order.*
>
> *Financial Statement for 1991/92*
>
> | | |
> |---|---|
> | *Income Salary* | *$40,000* |
> | *Rent from investment property* | *$8,320* |
> | *TOTAL INCOME* | *$48,320* |
> | *TOTAL DEDUCTIONS(Property Related)* | *$20,594* |
> | *TAXABLE INCOME* | *$27,726* |
> | *TOTAL TAX PAYABLE* | *$6,076* |
> | *(incl. Medicare)* | |
> | *APPROPRIATE FORTNIGHTLY INSTALMENTS* | *$234* |
>
> *Yours faithfully,*
>
> *John Citizen*

In the letter, you simply outline your salaried income, rental income and rental deductions and estimate your new taxable income. If you have any other income (e.g. interest) or other deductions (e.g. work related), these should also be included so that your overall financial position is presented. You may need to get an accountant to help you put in the figures but you don't need to be precise as any re-adjustment can be made at the end of the financial year, one way or the other. It is probably better to err on the side of the Tax Office, particularly as you will need to present this form at the end of every financial year.

In due course, you should expect to receive a letter back from the Taxation Office that might read something like this:

AUSTRALIAN TAXATION OFFICE
320 Adelaide St., Brisbane
Telephone: (07) 222 5011

OUR REFERENCE:
Contact Officer: Mr. I.M. Clerk

Mr J. Citizen
123 Paye St.,
Cleveland, 4163

Dear Mr Citizen,

INCOME TAX ....
YOUR LETTER DATED ....

In accordance with the provisions of Section 221D of the Income Tax Assessment Act 1936, as amended, authority is hereby given for tax instalment deductions required to be made from wages paid to you by
....
to be reduced ....
This authority remains in force from .... until ....
Please endorse this letter and hand it to your employer.

Yours faithfully,

....
Deputy Commissioner of Taxation

PART V

The Maintenance of Wealth

17 Financial Management

"An ounce of prevention is worth a pound of cure."

Old English Proverb.

Would you hop in the shower without first testing the water? I doubt it. Would you plan a shopping spree without first checking to see that you have enough money for what you want to buy? Probably not. And yet many people begin their journey to wealth without first taking all the precautions necessary to ensure their success. Building wealth through investment property means not only following the right principles, but also preparing for all eventualities *before* they happen. Most of the stories you hear about a tenant causing a landlord to sell his property and lose money are just that – stories. It's more likely that the investor was inept at managing his finances, struck financial difficulties and then blamed the tenant. Like the Scout's motto – be prepared. The unexpected always happens when you least expect it.

Debt management is just as important as property management. You need to develop confidence in handling debt and it's surprising how quickly you get to the stage where you learn to be very comfortable with debt because you can see and understand its power. Below is a check list of ideas that should help you to manage and master debt and protect your wealth building plan.

Budgeting

"Telling your money where to go instead of wondering where it went."

C.E. Hoover

It's important to prepare a budget every few months so that you keep an eye on all your incomings and outgoings – don't rely on intuition. And try to distinguish between essentials and luxuries. It's amazing how little the essentials in life actually cost. Rather than buy luxuries now, make a list of all you'll be able to buy later when you have achieved your goal.

Fix the interest rate

I am a great advocate of fixing the interest rate on loans no matter how high or low it may seem. It enables you to budget much more effectively. If you can afford to borrow the money at the interest rate offered, fix it for a minimum of three years, or longer if you feel the rate is particularly low. Taking a variable rate loan is potentially a recipe for disaster. At the time you take a loan, it may seem to you that interest rates couldn't possibly go higher. But the lessons of the 1990's have shown us that there is no upper limit to interest rates and investors who lost were those who were forced to sell because they couldn't keep up with the increased interest payments.

Interest-only

Taking an interest-only loan maximises your cash flow and gives you better tax advantages compared to a principal and interest loan. (For a principal and interest loan, the payment towards the principal is not tax deductible, and increases your loan payments unnecessarily). But if you feel more comfortable with a principal and interest loan, take it out for a long term (preferably 25 to 30 years), in which case, the principal and interest payment is almost all interest.

Section 221D

If you are a PAYE tax payer, it helps your cash flow if you write away to the Taxation Office in your state to get a variation on your regular tax instalments (see chapter 16). I don't see any point in waiting for up to two years for a tax refund when the increased amount in your pay packet can mean the difference between being strapped for cash or comfortable with your rental property. You can save around $1,000 on a $5,000 refund by claiming the reduction under 221D, instead of waiting for the refund.

Cash reserves

Always have sufficient cash reserves on hand to allow for unforeseen expenses. I believe that cash to the value of at least 5% of your total loans should be set aside for those unscheduled expenses (even if this money is borrowed with your loan). You should deposit the money in the name of the lowest-income earner to minimise the tax incurred on the interest. There's nothing like money in the bank to help you sleep better because you never know when emergencies will arise. Your ability to get your hands on money immediately can alleviate these temporary crises – maybe you can't do overtime this month, or your property may become vacant the same week you have to pay school fees.

Credit cards

As well as having some cash on hand, it is wise to open a few credit card accounts to provide additional access to funds – but don't use them to splurge on consumables for yourself. Have at least three or four cards with as high a credit limit as you can get, and make sure you pay them out early – before the "free credit" period is up.

Cheque-book mortgages

These types of overdraft facilities (explained in chapter 11) allow you to draw against an approved upper limit and repay the money at your convenience. These loans are great – not as long-term finance, but for immediate cash access. It may not be possible to have one of these loans early on (until you have two or three properties), because you won't have enough equity to utilise a conventional loan as well as a "cheque-book" loan. For this reason it is advisable to squeeze as much loan money from as few properties, so that eventually you have an unencumbered property to use in this way.

Assets:Liability ratio

Try to maintain your overall assets:liabilities ratio at 2:1. Although one particular property at any one time may have a high loan-to-value ratio, overall, the properties you have bought earlier should balance out the ratio to 2:1. This means that if you own $1 million worth of property, your total loans should be about $500,000 (net worth would also be $500,000). It doesn't matter if it's more or less at any particular stage (and it probably is less than this in the early stages), it's just a guide to help you keep your debt in perspective.

Unreliable income

Don't commit unreliable income to interest payments. For a two-income family, where there is the possibility that one might stop work in the near future (e.g. to start a family), do not commit both incomes to interest payments. If one member of the family intends working for three or four more years, you can still take advantage of this now, but make sure that the debt is manageable before that person stops work.

Speculation

By all means plan what you want to do when rents and wages increase, but never commit "maybe income" to interest payments. Although rents normally rise long-term in line with inflation, they may rise drastically some years and none in others. If you've had regular overtime for the last five years, then take this into account. Just take steps to ensure continuity of interest payments should the overtime suddenly stop.

Partnerships

Avoid partnerships where possible. Business deals with friends can be a good way to lose friends. I've seen many a good friendship torn apart by joint ventures into property investment. One wants to employ an agent, the other wants to rent it himself. One wants it repainted now, the other can't afford it. One loses his job and wants to sell because he hasn't taken adequate provisions for this happening, the other wants to buy him out and they can't agree on price. If a partnership is the only way you can get into property investment, then do it, but be aware of the pitfalls.

Vacancy rate

An acceptable vacancy factor is about 4%. This means that at any point in time, 4% of rentable properties are vacant, or alternatively, that your property is vacant for two weeks of the year on average. Too many investors expect 100% tenancy and become dismayed if the property lies vacant for more than a few weeks. Even if vacancy rates are higher than 4% - don't panic. Just remember that 30% of the population rent and that this percentage is increasing. So in times of high vacancy rates, there will still be tenants around, but they can afford to be choosy. Lowering the rent is a simple strategy to attract tenants but your contingency plan should also include having ready access to money. This can be achieved by any one of the many methods listed above. Reducing vacancies is as much about financial management as it is about property management and chapter 18 describes how vacancies can be reduced.

Rent insurance

There are quite a few innovative insurance policies around that cater for loss of rent for a set time. These cost a few hundred dollars, but in some cases, they also cover contents insurance for drapes and carpets etc. The insurance is tax deductible and a most worthy consideration if you are at all concerned by the effect of vacancies on your cash flow.

Mortgage repayment insurance

If you are at all concerned about job security or illness, you might consider taking out mortgage repayment insurance that will cover your mortgage repayment for a specified period if you are unable to work. This can be expensive, and it's probably cheaper to take other precautions, but if it means investing or not, do it.

Income replacement insurance

For self-employed people, loss of income through a downturn in the economy or some other factor is a justifiable worry. If you are in this situation, it is worthwhile considering an insurance policy that replaces at least part of your income should it cease. These policies can be costly but can offer great protection and the payment should be tax deductible.

Term life and disability insurance

No matter how secure your job, there's always the possibility that you will die or become incapacitated, leaving your loved ones with a lot of heavily negatively geared properties, and no income. It's reasonably inexpensive to take out life insurance for death and disability for an amount roughly equal to 15 times your salary. (If invested, this should provide an indexed income roughly equivalent to your present salary.) Don't forget to insure your spouse – too often it is the male who takes life insurance, with no cover for the spouse. This can cause untold hardship to the widower left to care for five school-age children with housekeeping and childminding fees. Take action before the unthinkable happens and don't skimp on life insurance. The cost of peace of mind can be very inexpensive.

Property insurance

Do not skimp on property insurance as it is important to minimise investment risk. Failure to be adequately insured can put a big hole in your finances. Make sure you take out insurance on the day you sign the contract, because if anything happens to the building between signing and settlement day, it is your loss. Building insurance should cover the replacement value as well as lost rent, demolition fees, architect's fees etc. Check that the insured value is a good 20% over what you think is the cost of the building. Contents insurance, which is usually taken out separately, should cover drapes and carpets if it is otherwise unfurnished. Also, as a courtesy, remind your tenants of their need to insure their personal contents.

Make a will

It's such a simple exercise to make a will and yet many people fail to do so. Perhaps we don't like to be pessimistic, however, a five minute exercise can avoid untold hardship if the inconceivable ever happens. It's amazing how many relatives turn up when you die intestate (without a will). You don't want to have an entire property portfolio thrust into the hands of someone else, such as the public trustee, for a lengthy term.

Knowledge

Financial worry is often caused by lack of knowledge. Keep up with the pursuit of knowledge – talk to as many other property investors as you can, read as much as you can and learn by your own experiences. Debt management is easy. The trick is to build a safety net beneath you so that if you ever falter, you don't go into free fall.

Property management

Managing your properties is but one element in successfully managing your finances and the following chapter should give you an insight into how this can best be achieved.

18
Property
Management

Building wealth through investment property enables you to have complete control over the management of your investment – but don't confuse management with involvement! Unfortunately, there are investors who feel they must be actively involved in everything that happens to their property – this often results in them selling because it "became too much of a hassle". These people think that they must save every last dollar to make their rental property work – they fix the washers, paint the walls, and collect the rent. But investment in property does not mean being personally responsible for every little incident. The returns from property can be so good that you can afford to pay someone to do the maintenance and management, and yet still achieve great results. For my part, I prefer to forego a *fantastic* return in favour of a *great* return by delegating the things I either don't enjoy or don't have time for, to someone else. I don't mind mowing and landscaping, but when it comes to painting, my limit is fences!

One aspect of property management I prefer to leave to someone else is dealing with the tenants. It is difficult to distance yourself and too easy to fall into the trap of becoming emotionally involved. I well remember the tenants in our very first investment property. In the early stages, the rent remained static, until eventually, it fell so far behind market rates, that it needed a 50% rise to bring it back into line. I didn't feel comfortable doing this, particularly since the tenants were struggling to keep up (mostly due to all their hire purchase commitments). Every year that passed (for 10 years I might add), I resolved that when these tenants left, I would raise the rent. But this was not to be. The tenants were now firmly entrenched and had no intention of moving – and indeed *could not afford* to move. Catch 22! After this experience, I prefer to use a professional property manager.

Whether you use a professional manager or not, you should consider the following points to maximise your returns and minimise the fuss.

Maintenance

Remember that it is your superannuation fund that you are running – don't let your property become run down or you'll find it eventually affects your payout at the end. Tenants dislike miserly landlords – especially those who collect the rent in a Porsche, yet refuse to fix a leaking roof. Good tenants are attracted to a property kept in good condition – and all your repair bills are tax deductible anyway. Well maintained properties are usually much easier to rent, which can be especially important at times when vacancies are high. One word of caution that needs repeating. Unless you enjoy being a handyman, don't try to do everything yourself. You'll find the property becomes an albatross around your neck, when it should be a wonderful vehicle for building wealth.

Improvements

Don't make the mistake of over-capitalising your property. If you want to add a third bedroom, work out the cost and judge whether it is justified in terms of the additional rent and recovery on sale. The most effective additions are outdoor living areas. Pergolas are inexpensive, increase the living area, and make the property more appealing to tenants.

Tenant screening

Contrary to popular belief, people with young children and pets often make good tenants. It has been my experience that, providing there is a clause in the contract for pets to be kept outside, tenants with pets can be just as fastidious as those without. Rather than try to choose tenants on the basis of such things as children, pets or marital status, it is far more important to select them according to their cleanliness and ability to pay. A reference from a previous landlord or employer, and a quick look at the last place of residence may be all that is required. Or you may need to run a credit check through one of the recognised credit agencies. Better still, get a good property manager to do the tenant screening for you.

Rent

You can collect the rent directly, have it deposited in any bank account, have it mailed to you, or allow an agent to do the same for you. Rent should be maintained at, or close to, the prevailing market rate, which is something with which an agent should be much more familiar. Don't fall into the trap of increasing the rent only once the tenants have left. The tenants will probably never leave because they're on such a good wicket, so you never get the chance to put the rent up. If there is a temporary over-supply of rental property, a slightly lower rent may mean fewer vacancies and should attract a larger number of tenants from which you can choose. Personally, I prefer to have fewer vacancies and a lower rent (80% of something is better than 100% of nothing).

Preparing leases

A lease protects both you and the tenant. A minimum of six months is standard and additional clauses can be added. The Real Estate Institute (REI) in your state has standard leases for use by real estate agents or you can obtain your own lease from a recognised stationer.

Handling arrears

Even though some rent money may be retrievable through the bond, prevention is better than cure – good tenant selection is critical. Having a good but firm relationship with the tenant may also solve any problem before it leads to a dispute. The first course of action is to approach the tenant tactfully because court action may prove costly to you and still may recoup no rent (if they don't have it, they can't pay it).

Advertising

Placing an advertisement in the local or State newspaper at least three to four weeks in advance will usually get a good response. Describe the property in an appealing way and be prepared to negotiate on the rent.

Vacancies

In many cases, clean, well maintained properties in handy locations and with a reasonable rent, should have a minimum of vacancies. Simply by following these few rules, you'll find tenants always attracted to your property and more inclined to stay longer. A good property manager should be able to advise you on how best to reduce vacancies, and they can usually have a new tenant lined up, just as one leaves.

Bond

This is usually four weeks rent and legislation in most states requires the bond to be placed with a Rental Bond Authority. Disputed bonds are probably the most frequent cause of concern for both landlords and tenants. Quite often the dispute arises from a simple misunderstanding that should have been clearly spelled out in the lease in the first place.

Inspections

These should be at least six-monthly but it certainly doesn't hurt to drive past your property more frequently. Keeping an eye on your property also gives you that feeling of security and a sense of being in control.

Relationship with tenants

Good property management is often about good people management. Tenants are an integral part of property investment and need to be treated with respect, not as second-class citizens. It is surprising how people respond to a little attention, but always maintain the relationship as one of professional courtesy.

Professional property management

If you decide to use a professional property manager instead of doing it yourself, you should take the trouble of finding a good one. This usually means finding a real estate agent who runs his rent roll as a business – not just as a sideline to his real estate sales. If need be, a property manager can do so much more than just collect the rent, organise the tradesmen and pay the rates and insurances. I have known my own property manager to dig a ditch to drain water away during a torrential downpour because he couldn't get anyone else at the time! The best property managers are usually very good people managers. Let me outline just some of the many reasons for using a professional property manager.

First and foremost, they provide the all important buffer between you and the tenant. Secondly, they are best placed to assess the appropriate rent and can ensure that it remains at market levels. In many cases they can find tenants more quickly and of a better quality than you can. They may not have to advertise as they have a lot of "walk in" enquiries and can personally screen the tenant. In times of high vacancies, a good property manager can "sell" a property to a tenant by pointing out all the property's advantages – in the same way as an agent sells a property to a buyer. A good property manager does not simply sign up the tenant on the dotted line of a lease. He takes special care to remind tenants of their commitments – this often prevents disputes arising in the first place. Usually the tenant is so eager to take up the tenancy, that they do not fully take in the extent of their obligations.

Like all other professions, property managers develop their own little tricks of the trade. Let me relate to you just one of the "secrets of property management" that my own property manager practices. He avails himself of every opportunity to check on the tenants without being intrusive. To this end, if a tenant rings up about a "spot of trouble", he always responds *immediately*. Now this gives him the opportunity to inspect the property "as is" (without the tenant doing a massive clean-up prior to a formal inspection) – and he knows the tenant is home. The tenant thinks he is great because the problem has been attended to immediately – and the landlord thinks he is great because he knows the property is being regularly inspected.

Never underestimate how important a good property manager can be to the success of your wealth building plans! It becomes increasingly important as your number of rental properties increase.

19
Learning from Others – Common Questions

Ultimately, building wealth is up to just one person – you. And the more you understand about property investment, the more confident you become in your decision making. Take the time to question and learn from others. Below is a list of the more common questions that have been asked during the various seminars that I have held. Perhaps you will identify with many of them.

What if I have no deposit for an investment property?

What you mean is that you have no cash deposit. Cash is not really necessary when you have equity in your own home. Having sufficient assets against which to borrow is all that is required and in this way, you can borrow the full amount plus all the additional costs.

Is property investment still OK if inflation is low?

It's not so much the absolute capital growth rate that is important, but rather the growth relative to inflation. With capital growth historically averaging between 2% and 4% over and above inflation, even if inflation were to fall, I would still expect property to perform at this level above inflation. In America, where annual inflation has been slightly lower at around 6%, property growth has averaged more than 8% per year, which is still that couple of percent above inflation.

Everything needs to be put in true perspective and if inflation, and consequently capital growth, is lower relative to everything else, property should still be better than any other form of investment. Furthermore, interest rates would have to fall, reducing the cost of the loan to such an extent that the overall rate of return (above inflation) on the property investment should remain about the same.

We own our own house but want to borrow money against this house to build a bigger and better house in which to live. We would still like to keep the one we're living in now as a rental property. Is the loan tax deductible?

The short answer is no, the loan is not tax deductible. This is a classic situation in which many property owners find themselves when they first decide to upgrade. Assessing whether interest on a loan is tax deductible depends on the *purpose* of the loan – not the *collateral* for the loan. In this case, the purpose of the loan is clearly to build a new home and not for the purpose of producing income. This situation is a double loss. Not only would the interest on the loan not be tax-deductible, but the rent from the investment property would be taxed at the highest marginal tax rate.

A simple solution could be to sell the first home and put the proceeds into the new home; you would then borrow to buy a rental property, using the equity in the new home as collateral. The interest on the loan would then be tax-deductible and instead of paying tax, a tax refund would more likely result.

However, there may be alternatives. For example, if the first home had been bought in the wife's name only, the husband could borrow the money to buy the property from his wife, and she could put the money she receives towards the new house. A legally binding contract is needed, and stamp duty must be paid, however, the tax benefits may far outweigh the transfer costs. I would recommend that you check with both your solicitor and accountant before you attempt any transaction of this nature.

What if the mortgage company goes bust?

You have their money so you cannot lose it in the same way as if the company has yours. The title of the property is in your name and at all times you have legal ownership. The mortgagee has no right of claim to your property – unless of course you reneg on your mortgage agreement. The only claim is on the money borrowed, not your property. Another financial institution may take over the defunct company or you may have the slight inconvenience and expense of refinancing elsewhere.

How do I pick the best area for capital growth?

Although it is human nature to want to find a bargain in an area of great capital growth, I believe it is false economy to spend a huge amount of time searching elsewhere for gems that are probably buried in your own backyard. It is virtually impossible, and really unnecessary, to guage just where the most valuable suburbs will be in the future. It is far more important to find an area that you know well rather than try to guess the area that has maximum capital growth potential. History has shown that reasonably well-located property should follow the pattern of around 10 to

11% capital growth over the long-term. If your property achieves better than this, it's more likely good luck than good selection. Rather than spending weekend after weekend driving from one side of the city to the other, you can maximise your returns and better manage your investment by organising your finances in the best possible way and ensuring that you pay only fair market value in an area around your home with which you are familiar. Of course, this may not always be achievable, particularly if you live in an expensive suburb and you find that you have to go further afield to find suitable rental property.

What if interest rates rise?

I personally recommend fixed-interest loans. If the rates rise, then you are insulated against rising repayments. On the other hand, if rates fall you should still be smiling. Have you noticed how low interest rates are usually followed by an increase in property prices? Also, if variable rates do rise, you are buffered by the tax refund.

Won't there be a glut of vacant properties when everyone discovers the advantages of owning rental property?

Firstly, let me remind you of the number of people who take any step towards becoming financially independent – there's such a small percentage of the population in the running to buy rental property. Secondly, people have been renting property since time eternal, and with more than 30% of the population renting, and this percentage increasing, tenants will not disappear overnight. There should always be a pool of tenants looking for rental accommodation and it's up to you to make your property most desirable.

Supply and demand in rental properties is cyclic and vacancies can and do occur from time to time. However, the baker doesn't expect to have customers in his shop every minute of the day from early morning until night and having a property vacant for a time is par for the course. But there are certain things you can do to keep this time to a minimum. Choosing the right property in the first place helps and well-located, well-maintained properties with reasonable rents attract more tenants.

I've been to several banks and they all say I can't afford an investment property. Where do I go from here?

It's quite common to find people turned down for a property investment loan, even though they feel sure they can afford it. Don't be disillusioned if your first approach to a bank is unproductive. It's up to you to prepare a budget and an assets/liabilities statement to not only assure yourself that you can do it, but also to assure the financier. In some cases, the financial institution won't have taken the tax refund into account, and this can make all the difference. Don't stop at the first "no". The great American baseballer Babe Ruth failed to get to first base just as many times as he hit a home run. Continue until you find a manager who will listen.

Most people seem to emphasise position, position, position. Should I buy prime residential property?

Property in prime locations does experience strong capital growth, perhaps slightly higher than normal, however the real return cannot be measured by the growth alone. There is not much point in purchasing a property one street back from the main shops if you have borrowed money using a principal and interest loan over 10 years with an interest rate of 18% and the property is so run down that nobody wants to rent it. I believe that property that is well-located, properly financed and properly managed will outperform property selected on the basis of position alone.

What if real estate prices stagnate?

Holding onto the house for at least 10 years should ensure a buffer against any cycles in the market. It's important to keep sight of long-term goals and not be distracted by any short-term hiccups. What happens to property values from one Christmas to the next should not concern you and although property can be cyclical, history shows that around 10% to 11% growth can be achieved long-term. More importantly, long-term property growth has performed at several percent above inflation.

Are units better than houses?

There is not a simple yes or no to this question. There are many financial factors to be considered as well as personal preferences. Houses may, and I say may, experience better capital growth because of the higher land content, but the maintenance could be higher and the yield (rent/value) could be lower. So in the longer term, the overall returns from units could be the same as for houses. Also, it's a case of horses for courses and the different tenant profile in some locations predetermines the suitability of houses, units or flats. Around the city centre, units or townhouses may suit the young professional couples whereas in the suburbs, young families might be more attracted to houses.

Do I have to get deeply involved if I invest in real estate?

No! Real estate is only the vehicle for building wealth – a means to an end and not the end itself. The great thing about property investment is that you can do as little or as much as you want to. You can do all the maintenance and bookwork yourself, or you can employ someone to do it all for you. The returns from property can be so great that you can afford to pay to have all those things done that you don't like doing or don't have time for – they're tax deductible anyway. A good property manager helps and he can do most things from paying the rates to arranging for the shower to be fixed or making insurance claims if necessary. The degree of involvement is entirely up to you. While doing everything yourself can increase your overall returns, weigh up the real cost in terms of family life and your peace of mind.

Shouldn't I buy upmarket real estate as an investment if I can afford it? Won't I get better capital gains?

Quite possibly you could get greater capital gains but the real rate of return in the long-term could be the same as, or lower than, a property in the lower end of the market. Just because a property valued at $100,000 might generate rent of $160 per week, it does not mean that a $500,000 property will rent for $800 per week. The rental market can only bear so much and in buying more expensive property, the market will dictate the rent you can command. Also there will be fewer people who can afford to pay the higher rent, so this will limit your choice of tenants. Another consideration is that the upper end of the property market is much more volatile and timing of the purchase becomes more critical.

I have $300,000 in equity in my own home. How much can I afford to borrow to buy more property?

It's not just a case of how much property you have to borrow against. It's just as important to consider your ability to service the loan. I have known people who own several million dollars worth of prime rural land, but because their income is limited, they are not capable of borrowing very much at all. No matter what the value of your properties, when it comes to borrowing money, we are generally limited by cash flow.

My wife and I live in a house worth $300,000. Would I be better to sell and buy a cheaper property in which to live and use the excess money to buy rental property? Or should I stay put and borrow against my home to buy more?

Economically speaking, you should downgrade and put the excess into rental property where you will be able to have more property working for you. However, when you are deciding just how much you want to invest, it's important to take personal considerations into account. You could live in a tent and own 10 investment properties or you can live in a mansion and have nothing else. Somewhere between the two extremes you'll find a happy medium.

I don't seem to have much spare money as it is now. How am I going to afford to buy an investment property?

If you have already made the commitment to pay for necessities first and luxuries last, then the only remaining stumbling block is more of a perceived problem than an actual problem. Too often, we think of an investment property in the same light as our first home. This being the case, we tend to see only the interest payment as creating an enormous burden. But your contribution to the interest bill, remember, is after the tenant and the taxman have paid their share, and what's left may be as little as $80 in the first year – and it gets less over time as the rents increase. In addition, section 221D of the Taxation Act may help you to improve your initial cash flow through reduced PAYE tax instalments which means you don't have to wait up to two years for your tax refund.

My wife isn't keen on the idea of buying an investment property in my name only. Is there an alternative?

There's not much point in putting a negatively geared property in joint names when the wife is not working, just in case of a marital break up. It is most tax advantageous to buy the property in the name of the highest-income earner. If you are at all worried about divorce, get a solicitor to draw up a written statement as to the equitable division of all your assets, regardless of title of ownership. This may only cost a small amount, compared to the thousands of dollars of potential tax savings.

Am I better off buying one property for $200,000 or two for $100,000?

Generally, it is better to buy more property at the cheaper price, but this depends entirely on the area in which you are buying. A $200,000 property in the inner city may be the bottom quarter of the market in that area, whereas a $200,000 property in a provincial town would probably be a mansion. In the former case, a $200,000 property would be OK but not so in the latter for a number of reasons. Firstly, a property in the lower end of the market has a higher rental yield, which results in a better cash flow. Secondly, the lower rent should attract more tenants. Thirdly, if you wish to sell on your retirement, there's more flexibility in selling one small property rather than one large one. And finally, if you're selling, property in the lower quarter of the market should attract other investors as well as first-home buyers, so there should be more potential purchasers.

Should I avoid timber houses because of the extra maintenance?

As an investment, timber houses can be just as good as brick houses. Usually they are cheaper than a brick equivalent, which may compensate for their maintenance later. Or if it is a very old house, it is quite possibly in a good position, being closer to the town centre – in which case, it may be more attractive to tenants or experience slightly greater capital growth that again compensates for the maintenance. But don't try to do all the maintenance yourself if you don't enjoy it. Too many landlords try to do everything themselves, instead of using tradesmen.

I've spent a long time looking for a good property but I seem to keep missing out on the real bargains. How long should I look before buying an investment property?

It's my opinion that the "once in a lifetime" bargain comes along about "once-a-month". However, try to remember the real costs in chasing a bargain. If you are investing longer-term, there's no need to spend six months of your valuable weekends in a real estate agent's car chasing that elusive bargain. Time heals all wounds, and so long as you pay fair market price (a little homework should determine what this value would be), you should still achieve sound capital growth. Don't buy the first property you come across, but on the other hand, don't go out with any preconceived ideas of what makes the perfect investment property because you'll spend a year looking for something that may not exist. Spend at least a month familiarising yourself with values in your area, so that when you do find that "right" property, you'll immediately recognise it.

With an interest-only loan, when do I actually get to own the property?

While it is true that, with an interest-only loan, there is a perpetual debt on the property, you retain title to the property at all times. Whether you ever get to "own" the property outright is irrelevant. What is important is your equity in the property and how fast it increases over time. Eventually the debt will be insignificant compared to the property value. Reducing the principal reduces the interest claimable and you'll then pay tax on the rent. So why pay it out? The only loans you should pay out while you are building wealth are those that are not tax deductible – such as the loan on your own home or car.

What if a consumption tax (Goods and Services Tax – GST) is introduced and personal tax rates are cut. Will this affect property investment?

Initially, the value of most commodities will rise causing an increase in property values. This is because both land development costs and building materials will increase, directly affecting property values. Longer term, although the tax effectiveness will be marginally less, everything is relative and all other tax-advantaged investments will be similarly affected. If residential property outperforms all other investments now, then there is no reason to expect that this will be any different with a consumption tax.

What if negative gearing is abolished?

The government has already made the mistake of abolishing the right to claim interest losses from rental property against other income. The turmoil in the rental market that occurred when investors took flight was so great, that it was reintroduced within two years. I believe the government is unlikely to make the same mistake twice. But in the unlikely event that it does, I wouldn't expect the change to be retrospective and it would be a matter of adjusting the debt to balance the rental income.

Will they ever get rid of the capital gains tax?

Revenue from the capital gains tax is now firmly entrenched in the government's budget. Since it was introduced in 1985, billions of dollars have been collected as a direct result of the tax and to remove it now would mean drastic cuts to sensitive areas such as education and health. For this reason, I believe it is here to stay. However, it is not the bogey it is made out to be and it should not really affect long-term investors. If you don't sell, you don't pay and because it applies only to gains above inflation, it is usually minimal if you do sell in the long-term. The tax was intended to encourage long-term investment and discourage short-term speculators – and this it does very effectively.

I knew someone who had a fantastic business as an owner-driver of a concrete truck. He purchased two investment properties but when the recession came, his business declined and the banks foreclosed on the mortgage. Does this mean that buying rental property is only for those with a secure income and not for the self-employed?

What is a secure income? No job is 100% safe and the precautions you take with your investment properties are commensurate with the degree of risk you attach to your current employment. For example, a government employee with a seemingly "secure" job may only need to have cash in the bank, access to a lot of credit cards and a "check-book" type mortgage. On the other hand, a self-employed truck driver should take all the above steps as well as disability insurance, income replacement insurance and possibly mortgage repayment insurance. Don't let the prospect of losing your job prevent you from undertaking a loan for a rental property. Simply take all the necessary precautions in case the unexpected happens.

Is a holiday unit at the coast a good investment?

It can be if you are careful to distinguish between an investment and a luxury. If purely for investment, the returns can be as good as permanent lettings if it is let for half the year at twice the normal rental. This means that you use the unit when it is not let rather than letting it when you are not using it. If however, you want it solely for your own holidays thinking it will serve as an investment as well – think again. None of the expenses (including interest) is tax deductible so it could be an expensive luxury. By the time you have created your wealth, you should well be able to afford a luxurious holiday unit that you can use at any time you so desire.

We were brought up to believe that we shouldn't borrow money. Were Mum and Dad wrong?

Yes and no! The golden rule of borrowing money is to borrow for appreciating assets such as property, not for consumables that depreciate in value. Our parents were right in deterring us from borrowing money for cars etc, which ultimately are worthless. However, no one bothered to explain to them that debt, if used for appreciating assets such as property, is a most important tool in building wealth.

Why hasn't my accountant told me everything about investing in property?

When you go to the garage for petrol, does the mechanic come running out to suggest that your brakes need checking or that it's time for a tune up? We probably expect too much of accountants. They should be able to answer all of your questions competently, but don't expect them to be creative in guiding your wealth creation program. Accountants are usually specialists in their area of expertise – accounting. They will expertly complete the tax forms for you after you have provided them with all the figures. They are usually not specialists in property investment and should never be relied on as such. However, there are some accountants who do specialise in property – and even have some rental property of their own.

We seem to be in the middle of a recession. Is it still a good time to buy rental property?

The herd mentality of the population is such that everyone buys when everyone else is buying and sells when everyone else is selling. (Statistics show that most investors bought in the midst of the last property boom when interest rates and property prices were at their highest!!) Successful investors look on a downturn in the economy as a great time to buy and they then take all the necessary steps to ensure that they are able to hold long-term to reap the rewards of future recovery.

Should I buy a property in partnership with a friend?

Usually, this is one sure recipe to lose a friend. If the investment is worthwhile, do it yourself. Different people will have different ideas on investments. However, if it is the only way that you can afford to get started in property investment, then have a go, but beware of the pitfalls.

20
Learning More –
A Reading List

*"It is the tragedy of this world that no one knows what he doesn't know –
and the less a man knows, the more sure he is that he knows everything."*

Joyce Cleary

The most effective way of learning is through personal experience but believe me this can be very, very expensive. However, by reading books, learning can be through the experience of others and is just the cost of a book. Unfortunately, 80% of books are read by 20% of people and many do not appreciate the wealth of knowledge available.

Reading and learning from others is a great start towards becoming a successful property investor and the more you read, the more likely you are to become your own expert. I regularly buy one or two books a week and consider my library as one of my greatest investments.

Successful property investors are usually characterised by three traits:

• *They have sound financial principles.*
• *They are highly motivated to succeed.*
• *They divert their energies and money into property investment.*

With these three characteristics in mind, a recommended reading list is outlined below together with some personal comments I have made regarding the information contained in these books.

Financial Principles

"Making Money Made Simple" by Noel Whittaker (Simon & Schuster) 1987

Highly recommended and a great starting point even for teenagers. The basic principles of handling money are explained in very simple terms. A must for everyone.

"More Money with Noel Whittaker" by Noel Whittaker (Simon & Schuster) 1990

This is a very large reference book about all types of investments, but it does display a greater emphasis towards managed funds. The author's style of writing projects a very positive image about investing and should provide you with the encouragement to at least do something about improving your financial status.

"Getting it Together" by Noel Whittaker (Simon & Schuster) 1993

An absolute must for all young people - and some older ones as well with young children.

"The Three R's of Investing" by Austin Donnelly (Allen and Unwin Australia Pty Ltd) 1985

This and other books by the same author, "More Wealth with Less Risk" and his latest "More Wealth Through Beating The Money Traps" are very comprehensive and contain a lot of useful information about the pitfalls relating to investing. The only disappointing aspect is that the author writes more on what not to do than on what to do. It was not clear to me exactly what he *would* recommend in the way of investments.

"Unlimited Success in Personal Investments" by Don Stammer (Wrightbooks) 1989

A good summary of the many options available. Although it is not particularly detailed, it makes very good light reading.

"Daryl Dixon's Guide to 161 Tax and Investment Strategies" by Daryl Dixon (Information Australia Group) 1988

Lots of information relating to taxation and investments and many thought-provoking suggestions.

"Tax Forms and Refunds – Made Easy" by Information Australia (Edited by S.A. Block and W.L. Williams) 1989

A very easy book to read on all taxation matters. Takes a very non-conservative approach.

"Money Success and You" by John Kehoe (Zoetic Inc) 1990

This is a great book and emphasises that your attitude to wealth plays an over-riding role in building wealth. Most certainly a book to boost your confidence.

"Financially Free" by Anne Hartley (Doubleday) 1990

Highly recommended. Although directed at women, it is a good book for all to read and stresses the importance of good attitudes and habits in the quest for prosperity.

Motivation to Succeed

"Think and Grow Rich" by Napoleon Hill (Wilshire Book Company) 1966. (First published in 1937)

A highly motivating book written over 50 years ago in a very simple and easy to read style. Still very relevant today and a must to read.

"The Greatest Success in the World" and "University of Success" by Og Mandino (Bantam Books) 1981

Og Mandino's books are very short and his classic story-telling method is inspirational in identifying the principles of success.

"Power to Choose" by Haydn Sargent (Boolarong Publications) 1989

A wonderful book, very simply written and suitable for all ages. It deals with self-motivation and success and will give you loads of self-confidence.

"The 7 Habits of Highly Effective People" by Stephen R. Covey (Information Australia) 1990

This book is outstanding. It covers the principles of success in such graphic detail that you cannot help but be influenced by his powerful ideals. The book is rather lengthy and it would be very nice to see it summarised into a smaller booklet so that its message would reach a greater audience.

Property Investment

"Riches from Real Estate" by Fred Johnson and Brendan Whiting (Fredan Pty Ltd) 1979

A must for all. A well written, easy to follow book that espouses the simple but effective philosophy of "always buy and never sell". If you read nothing else, read this! Earlier books by the same authors are:

"How to Get Real Estate Rich"

"More Riches from Real Estate"

"New Ways to Real Estate Wealth"

"New Ways to Real Estate Wealth in New Zealand"

"The Way Ahead to Property Wealth"

Unfortunately, these books are now out of print so if you come across one in the library or via a real estate agent or investor who's been around for a while, grab at the chance to read them.

"Unlimited Success in Real Estate" by Christopher Lang (Brooks Waterloo Publishers) 1986

A very light reading book. Lots of good ideas, together with stories of the author's own experiences. The emphasis is on creative thinking.

"Unlimited Success in Property Development" by Christopher Lang (Brooks Waterloo Publishers) 1989

Short and sweet but with some innovative ideas on investing. Worthwhile reading if only for the lateral thoughts.

"Unlimited Success in Acquiring Investment Property" by Christopher Lang (Wrightbooks Pty Ltd) 1991

A bit of a rehash of the first two books but never-the-less, it contains a few new excellent ideas about property investment.

"The Residential Property Report – Australian Capital Cities" by BIS Shrapnel Pty Ltd

This report is published annually and is available through BIS Shrapnel directly. Although quite expensive (around $300 per year), I believe the information contained in this series of reports is extremely well researched and invaluable to not only industry groups, but also to those property investors who are interested in the research behind the facts. It covers all aspects of capital growth and rents dating back to the sixties for all the Australian Capital Cities and contains forecasts of future trends. Address: BIS Shrapnel, 7th Floor, Norplaza, 169 Miller St, North Sydney, 2060. Telephone: (02) 959 5924.

"Market Facts" – Real Estate Institute of Australia Ltd

This is a monthly review of the major residential property markets in Australia and gives you an up-to-date picture of price and rent movements in all the major cities. The cost is approximately $200 per year. Address: REIA, P.O. Box 234, Curtin, ACT, 2605. Telephone: (O6) 282 4277.

"How to use your HOME EQUITY to invest in a second house – and a third" by Lois Towart (Book Works Pty Ltd) 1989

A very good book if you're just starting out and it gives a great overall picture of property investment. Her latest release entitled "Your Home Equity Can Make You Rich" is an expanded version of her first book, but with additional chapters touching on finance and tax.

"Investing in Real Estate" by Alan J. Falkson (Book Works Pty Ltd) 1989

This book is a collection of stories and examples of how to trade, not invest, in property and he takes an extremely aggressive approach to buying and selling property. An update of this book entitled "Investing in

Real Estate on a Budget" is an expanded version of the first book and again is a collection of ideas on trading. Read it if only for the motivation – for he certainly writes with enthusiasm.

"Investing in Residential Property – Understanding the Market" by Peter Waxman and Dennis Lenard (The Alliance Publishing Group) 1988

A well worthwhile book although a little heavy going. It does not tell you how to invest in residential property but concentrates on presenting the statistics for you to interpret. Contains some excellent material.

"Tax Driven Real Estate Strategies" by Les Szekely and Anthony Cordato (The Investment Library) 1991

A very up-to-date and extremely comprehensive book, especially regarding the tax implications of property investment. It covers all aspects of both commercial and residential properties and although it offers no specific wealth building strategies, it is a most useful reference book.

"Queensland Development Report" by Rider Hunt

This is an excellent publication. The quarterly report costs around $100 per year and contains a huge amount of statistical data pertinent to all types of development including population movement figures and property sales surveys. Contact Telephone: (075) 38 3099.

"Creating Wealth" by Robert G. Allen (Simon and Schuster) 1983

An American book that again promotes the idea of accumulating residential property as a life-long investment. This is a great book if you can overlook the fact that American financing techniques are entirely different to those in Australia. Another book by the same author "Nothing Down" (Simon and Schuster), relies quite heavily on creative financing techniques applicable only in America. It is based on acquiring apartment blocks in the USA with no cash deposits (nothing down).

"How to Make it When You're Cash Poor" by Hollis Norton (Simon and Schuster) 1985

Very similar to the Robert Allen books. Emphasis is on the creative finance methods of purchasing houses with no cash deposits. These American books make great reading, despite the differing finance methods, because the authors exude optimism.

Appendix:
Property Investment Analysis by Computer

Working out the rate of return on any investment is basically a matter of analysing what you put in compared to what you get back at the end. In the very simple case of cash invested in a bank, what you put in are the deposits and what you get back at the end will be the sum these deposits plus the interest accrued each year, less the tax you pay. The rate of return is effectively the interest rate that the bank offers minus the tax you would have to pay at your marginal rate.

With property investment, the rate of return is still calculated from what you put in compared to what you get back. However, the equations are much more complicated than those for cash in a bank. For a property where you have a large initial deposit, what you get back would be the positive annual after-tax cash flows plus equity build-up in the property. Where you have little or no initial cash deposit, the annual after-tax cash flows (interest minus net rent plus tax refund) would be negative. In this case, what you put in would be your annual contributions to cover this deficit, while what you get back would simply be the equity build up. The real rate of return is effectively the "interest rate" that you would have to receive on these after-tax contributions to attain the equity at the end. This percentage is termed the internal rate of return (IRR).

Understanding Internal Rate of Return for a Negatively Geared Property

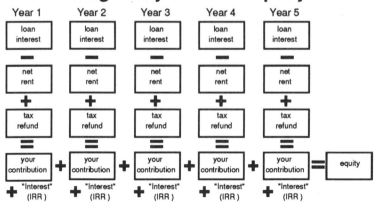

To estimate the rate of return on a property in advance, you must make some assumptions and projections for all the factors that determine your after-tax costs (these will change each year) and the growth in value of the property. The internal rate of return (IRR) is then calculated by trial and error such that the sum of your annual "deposits" plus the "interest" each year is equal to the equity at the end. To see how this works, let's look at a specific example of a $100,000 property and to make it easy, all the relevant figures are set out in a spreadsheet below. Although it *is* possible to calculate the internal rate of return from such a property manually, the number of factors that need to be considered together with the tediousness of using a trial and error method make the use of a computer program very attractive. In fact, the spreadsheet layout that I have used comes directly from a computer program that I developed for this specific purpose.

Property Investment Analysis (PIA)

	Assumptions	1992	1993	1994	1995	1996	1997
1	Property Value	$100,000	111,000	123,210	136,763	151,807	168,506
2	Purchase Costs	2,700					
3	Deposit	$0					
4	Loan	$104,500	104,500	104,500	104,500	104,500	104,500
5	Equity	-$4,500	6,500	18,710	32,263	47,307	64,006
6	Capital Growth	11%					
7	Inflation Rate	8%					
8	**Gross Rent/wk/yr**	$160	8,320	8,986	9,704	10,481	11,319
9	**Cash Deductions**						
10	Loan Interest	14%	14,630	14,630	14,630	14,630	14,630
11	Property Expenses	20%	1,664	1,797	1,941	2,096	2,264
12	**Pre-Tax Cash Flow**	$0	-7,974	-7,442	-6,866	-6,245	-5,575
13	**Non-Cash Deductions**						
14	Depreciation - Building	2.5%	1,300	1,300	1,300	1,300	1,300
15	Depreciation - Fittings	$6,000	1,200	960	768	614	492
16	Borrowing Costs	$1,800	600	600	600		
17	**Total Deductions**	$0	19,394	19,287	19,239	18,641	18,685
18	**Tax Credit (actual)**	47.25%	4,667	4,619	4,505	3,859	3,524
19	**After-Tax Cash Flow**	$0	-3,307	-2,823	-2,361	-2,386	-2,051
20	**Rate of Return - IRR**	63.8%	per year				
21	Before Tax Return	121%	per year				

Notes on spreadsheet

The figures under the 1992 heading (in bold) represent the inputs and assumptions used to calculate the projections of the following five years. Although this particular analysis is over 5 years, the same process can be used to calculate the rate of return over any number of years. The notes that follow describe these variables and correspond to the numbers on the left hand side of the spreadsheet. Each item of the spreadsheet is described in terms of the figures used in this particular example and alternative entries are suggested.

1. Property value

The $100,000 property value in this example represents the price paid for the property and is assumed to increase each year at a constant rate of compound growth. However, if renovations were carried out immediately after purchase, this could directly affect the property value and its potential for capital growth. Renovations may affect the property value but not the stamp duty that is paid on the original purchase price. Also, if furniture is bought in addition to the property, the furniture costs will not necessarily be part of the property value considerations. However, they may increase the size of the loan if you have borrowed to buy them as well as increasing the depreciation claims.

2. Purchase costs

These include state government stamp duty and your solicitor's fees. In this case, stamp duty is assumed to be $2,350 (Qld rates for a $100,000 property) and solicitor's fees $350, giving total purchase costs of $2,700. Although the stamp duty is a fixed amount, solicitor's fees may vary from firm to firm or you may not even use one.

3. Deposit

The "deposit" represents the total amount of cash outlaid at the time of purchase. In this case, it is assumed that there is no cash deposit and that the total loan covers both the purchase price and all associated purchase and borrowing costs. The size of the deposit that you may wish to make will affect the size of the loan and consequently your cash flow. Small deposits produce negative cash flows and usually produce large tax benefits – while large deposits will produce positive cash flows and usually incur large tax liabilities. The initial deposit, in either case becomes the first item in the after-tax cash flow analysis.

4. Loan

This is simply the total of all costs (property price, purchase costs, loan costs etc.) less the amount of the deposit. In this case, as the deposit is nothing, the loan of $104,500 represents the total of all costs. If renovations were carried out immediately, or if the property was a holiday unit that required furniture, the loan may include these costs as well. The loan in this example is interest-only, and consequently, the debt remains constant for the entire five years. If a principal and interest loan was used, the debt would decrease with time until eventually the equity would be the total value of the property.

5. Equity

This is the difference between the property value and the debt on the loan. The equity increases in line with the increasing value of the property and for a principal and interest loan, with the decreasing debt. In the example, the loan was interest-only and so the equity of $64,006 after five years was solely due to the capital growth. Obviously, paying out the principal will increase the equity faster, but in fact, it decreases the rate of return because you have to put in more of your own money, and receive less tax benefits. Sales commission and capital gains tax have not been deducted here, but it is possible to do a separate calculation taking these into account.

6. Capital growth

This is the expected long-term annual compound rate of growth in the value of the property (assumed to be 11% in the example). Although it is assumed to increase uniformly, the end result is not affected if the rate has varied over the time. What is important in the calculation is the end value of the property, not what has happened to the value along the way. As a result, the property may increase in value only in the final year, and the return would be the same as if growth was uniform.

7. Inflation rate

This is the expected long-term rate of inflation (assumed to be 8% per year in the example). Increases in rent and property expenses (rates, insurance, etc) are assumed to increase at this rate. If capital gains tax is to be considered, the inflation rate will also affect the actual taxable gain because the property value will be indexed to inflation.

8. Gross rent (/week and /year)

The first cell contains the expected weekly rent, while the rest of the row represents the corresponding annual rent calculated simply as the weekly rent times 52, and is assumed to increase each year in line with inflation. In contrast to the capital growth application to the property value, the regularity of increases in rent can affect the rate of return. This is because rents directly affect cash flows each and every year. Yet another consideration at this point is whether or not there are potential vacancies to be accounted for. These will affect the yearly rent projections.

9. Cash deductions

These differ from "non-cash deductions" in that they are real cash outflows. Cash deductions consist of loan interest and rental expenses.

10. Loan interest

The first cell represents the interest rate while the rest of the row represents the corresponding annual interest payments. In this example, the loan is assumed to be fixed-rate (14%), interest-only and so the interest payments are a constant $14,630 each year. However, with a principal and interest loan, the interest component of the payment each year would decline so that although the loan payment remains constant for the period of the loan, the tax benefits would be reduced over time. Also, with a principal and interest loan, the payment towards the principal would need to be accounted for separately, as it directly affects the cash flow and the equity but not the tax refund.

11. Expenses

These include the costs of rates, insurances and maintenance etc, but exclude the interest on the loan. In the example, it has been calculated simply as a fixed percentage (20%) of the annual gross rent and which increases with inflation. But these expenses might vary depending on the maintenance and whether or not you manage the property yourself.

12. Pre-tax cash flow

This is what flows in or out of your pocket before tax is taken into account. It is calculated as the gross rent less loan payments and expenses. If you have an interest-only loan, as in the example, the loan payment equals the interest payment. But for a principal and interest loan, the loan payment is part principal payment and part interest payment.

13. Non-cash deductions

The three types of tax deductions that indirectly affect your cash flow in the form of tax benefits are "depreciation" on the building, depreciation on the fittings, and the loan or borrowing costs. They can significantly affect your cash flow and are often the forgotten items in property investment analysis. These do not affect the actual costs of expenses and interest, but they do affect the overall "loss" and consequently the tax benefits.

14. "Depreciation" on building

This capital allowance is based on the initial construction cost of the building. In this example, the construction cost was $52,000, and the depreciation rate was 2.5% ($1,300) each year for 40 years. The allowance may be 0, 2.5% (over 40 years) or 4% (over 25 years) and depends on *when* the property was constructed. Although it adds tax benefits, it is not the sole criterion for choosing between a new or established property.

15. Depreciation on fittings

In this example, the cost of the fittings was assumed to be 6% of the property value, and the amount claimed for depreciation was 20% on a diminishing scale. The prime cost method of depreciation may be used, but the diminishing value method confers tax benefits sooner and is thus more tax effective.

16. Borrowing costs

In this example, the costs are spread over 3 years. As a result, the tax benefits are noticeably reduced in the fourth year causing an increase in the after-tax cash flow in that year. It is possible for these borrowing costs to be written off over 5 years, depending on the term of the loan.

17. Total deductions

This is the sum of all deductions claimed – both cash and non-cash and in the example, amount to $19,394 in the first year. These deductions decline over the first few years, despite the fact that expenses rise with inflation. This is because the borrowing costs and depreciation claims (under the diminishing value method) are initially high. After about eight years, the deductions increase in line with the additional expenses.

18. Tax credit

The first cell represents the marginal tax rate (47.25% in this example), and the rest of the row is the annual tax credit. There are two ways of calculating the tax credit. The easiest method is simply to assume that the entire loss (rent less deductions) occurs within the one marginal tax rate. This gives a reasonable approximation but a more precise method requires a knowledge of the exact taxable income. The precise method of using taxable income ($40,000 not shown) has been used in the example. If a large deposit had been used on the property, then the property would more than likely produce a profit, in which case, the items in this row would represent the tax liabilities.

19. After-tax cash flow

This is the amount of cash invested in or gained from the property each year. In this example, the after-tax cash flow is negative in which case it represents the investment or contribution ($3,307 in the first year). This should decrease with time as rents rise with inflation. Eventually a point would be reached where the rents overtake the loan payments and property expenses. At this time, there is a positive after-tax cash flow. It is possible to borrow the negative after-tax cash flows so that in effect, the property costs you nothing! I don't recommend this procedure, but it certainly presents an interesting mathematical concept. It is the after-tax cash flows that are used to calculate the internal rate of return – IRR.

20. IRR

This is the after-tax rate of return on all moneys invested in or gained from the property over the period considered. In the property investment example, the figures involved in the IRR calculation are the after-tax cash flows each year, together with the equity after 5 years.

Assumptions	1992	1993	1994	1995	1996	1997
5 Equity						64,006
19 After-Tax Cash Flow	$0	-3,307	-2,823	-2,361	-2,386	-2,051

These after-tax cash flows represent your contribution to the property each year and could be considered as the deposits made into a bank account. If, after five years, there is $64,006 in equity, then the interest rate needed to produce this result would have had to have been 63.8% – which is the internal rate of return or IRR. There are many variations that can occur with these cash flows. For example, if there is a cash deposit, then this becomes the cash flow in the very first year. And if the deposit is large enough, the subsequent annual after-tax cash flows all become positive.

The rate of return on a negatively geared property will gradually decline with time. In the particular example used, the IRR after 5 years is 63.8%, but if the same calculations were carried out over a 10 year period, the IRR would be 37%. The reasons for this are twofold. Firstly, because rents rise with time, the tax benefits diminish to the point where tax is paid. Secondly, the equity in the property is substantially increased with time so the leverage effect on your money is reduced. In the first year, your gearing ratio (property value to equity is $104,500 to 0 (if that is possible) but after 5 years it is $168,506 to $64,006 (almost 3:1) and after 10 years it is $283,942 to $179,442 – about 2:1.

After a very long time (more than 25 years), the IRR would be reduced to around 15%, which is effectively the capital growth plus net after-tax yield from the property. To maintain an overall higher rate of return, further properties should be bought when cash flow permits. This will regain the tax benefits and increase the overall gearing ratio.

21. Pre-tax equivalent

This is the interest rate that your bank would have to pay if you were to get an equivalent rate of return! In this case, with a marginal rate of 47.25%, the rate would have to be 121%.

Sensitivity Analysis

It is important to understand the effect of changes in the various inputs on the rate of return, and using the computer program, it is possible to do a sensitivity analysis to look at all the "what ifs" of property investment. The examples in the table below show the sensitivity of the IRR over 5 years to changes in some assumptions used in the previous spreadsheet.

Sensitivity Analysis

Change to Inputs	Cost per wk 1st Yr	IRR per yr
No Change	$64	63.8%
Inc. $30,000	$76	55.3%
Inc. $30,000, Exp. 30%	$88	48.1%
Inc. $30,000, Exp. 30%, Grth 8%	$88	31.1%
Inc. $30,000, Exp. 30%, Grth 8%, Dep. $20,000	$47	18.1%

As you can see from the table, the rate of return is very sensitive to the deposit size with large deposits lowering the IRR. Contrary to what many people believe, rates of return are not greatly affected by such factors as rental expenses, primarily because the impact of these is lessened as a result of the corresponding tax credits. From the table above, you can also see how the weekly cost varies with the changing assumptions.

Property Comparisons

Property investors are always keen to get the maximum return on their property, but too often it is just the capital growth or the rental return that is considered. I would like to show you how at first glance, figures can be misleading. Using the computer program, I can demonstrate that totally different properties may still have the same internal rate of return.

In a hypothetical situation, let's compare three properties, all of which cost $100,000 and all of which return 37%. This cost is arbitrary as the exercise is simply to show you how important it is to take all factors into account before purchasing any property. The first property could be a new suburban brick house with rent at $160 per week; the second could be a pair of flats with total rent at $220 per week and the third could be an older inner city dwelling with rent at $170 per week. For each property, there was no deposit and the interest on the loan of $104,500 (including all costs) was 14%. It was also assumed that the investor's income was $40,000 per year. The table on the next page shows you the picture.

Comparing Rates of Return (IRR) After 10 Years

	Pair of Small Flats Near Inner City	New Outer Suburban Brick House	Old Renovated Inner City Property
Initial Value	$100,000	$100,000	$100,000
Value at 10 Yrs	$259,374	$283,942	$339,457
Equity at 10 Yrs	$154,874	$179,442	$234,957
Capital Growth	10%	11%	13%
Rent per Week	$220	$160	$170
Property Exp.	30%	20%	30%
Wkly Cost 1st Yr	$58	$64	$80
IRR per Yr	**37%**	**37%**	**37%**

Despite the differences in the various factors such as growth and rent, after 10 years, the internal rate of return on each property was 37% per year. Why is this so? Why can three totally different properties give the same returns? The answer lies in the combination of *all* the factors such as capital growth, rent, vacancies, depreciation and maintenance and other expenses. It is possible that flats, having lower land content, have normal 10% capital growth and although the rent of $220 represents a good yield, it is highly likely that vacancies and maintenance would be higher because of the nature of the flats and the type of tenant they usually attract.

On the other hand, a new brick house in suburbia may have a 2.5% building allowance that provided some additional tax benefits. Apart from this, the property probably experiences growth of 11 % with average rent (at $160 per week), minimum vacancies and low maintenance. This would result in an outlay of $64 per week in the first year. At the other end of the spectrum, an older style inner city house may experience strong capital growth because of the scarcity factor of inner city property, but may need a lot of ongoing maintenance.

Basically it boils down to the more money you put in along the way, the more you get out at the end. And as you can see from the table on the previous page, the older property may cost you initially $80 per week in return for greater capital gains at the end while the flats may cost much less at $58 per week for less capital gains at the end. This is not a reason for suggesting that one investment is better than another, but simply that one investment suits one particular person more than another. But be careful, it is not meant to suggest that all properties worth $100,000 will return 37%.

Computer Programs *PIA (Property Investment Analysis)*

The company's PIA computer program was developed to help people answer their own "what ifs" about property investment. It comes in two versions, one for investors, and one for professionals wishing to assist clients. Both are available for either IBM compatible or Macintosh personal computers. PIA is extremely powerful, yet very easy to use.

PIA Advanced Personal

The PIA Advanced Personal program was designed specifically for property investors to help them calculate capital growth, cash flows and rates of return (IRR) on investment properties. It takes account of the tax situation to calculate the investor's precise financial commitment.

The program will compute cash flow projections for up to 40 years and has the facility for changing more than 100 variables including property price, rent, capital growth, inflation, deposit, etc. There is extensive on-line help with simplified auxiliary data-entry screens, where the variables can be broken down into individual components. It is possible to evaluate alternative loan types (e.g. interest-only versus principal and interest or combinations of both), to examine the effects of buying a property in single or joint names (including varying percentage splits), and even to assess the cash flows and rates of return on a portfolio of properties.

As well as answering all the investor's "what ifs", it can be used to prepare a detailed financial report for the accountant and bank manager.

PIA Professional

PIA Professional was designed for professionals such as accountants, real estate agents and financiers to enable them to demonstrate the financial aspects of investment property to investors.

In addition to all the features of the Advanced Personal version, it has comprehensive graphics screens (e.g. property value vs debt, cash flow break even, fixed interest comparisons, etc), an extensive range of property and finance calculators for answering investors questions (e.g. retirement ready reckoner, loan consolidation and eligibility, capital gains tax, etc) and produces more detailed client-oriented reports.

An important feature of the Professional version is its ability to simulate home loans and to analyse the effect of linking them with loans associated with an investment property.

PIA Professional is part of a package which includes the two *Building Wealth* books and the video. It also includes a site licence which enables the program to be used on more than one computer within the one office.

ORDER FORM

PLEASE SEND ME :

Computer Program: *PIA Advanced Personal* $129 [   ]

                    PIA Professional $475 [   ]

DISK SIZE: 5.25" [   ] 3.5" [   ]   *VERSION:* Mac [   ] Windows [   ]

Book: *Building Wealth in Changing Times* $29 [   ]

Book: *Building Wealth through Investment Property* $29 [   ]

Video: *Building Your Wealth through Investment Property* $49 [   ]

TOTAL AMOUNT   [$]

(All Prices Include Postage & Handling)

PLEASE NOTIFY ME:

We are continually producing and updating software and other material relating to property investment. If you want to be informed of any new or updated material, please tick the box.   [   ]

Mr/Mrs/Ms_____ First Name _____

Surname _____

Address_____

_____

_____ State _____ P'code _____

Phone No. _____ I enclose a cheque [   ] or please

Debit my Bank Card [   ] Master Card [   ] Visa Card [   ] for $ _____

No |__|__|__|__|__||__|__|__|__|__||__|__|__|__||__|__|__|__| Exp __ / __

Card Holder's Signature _____

Please post, phone or fax your order to:

Somerset Financial Services Pty Ltd   Telephone   (07) 3286 4368
P.O. Box 615, Cleveland Qld. 4163.   Fax: (07) 3821 2005

(To preserve the quality of this book, the order form may be photocopied)